Letters to the daughter I'll never have

Ashley Brown

MEZCALITA
PRESS

MEZCALITA PRESS, LLC
Norman, Oklahoma

Cover Design: Christopher Everett
Cover Painting: Norma Brown

MEZCALITA PRESS, LLC
Norman, Oklahoma

Letters to the daughter I'll never have

Ashley Brown

Table of Contents

I think we dream so we don't have to be apart for so long. If we're in each other's dreams, we can be together all the time.

~ A.A. Milne

Prologue

Fifty-three minutes into a fifty-five minute counseling session, which we'd devoted fully to the question I'd been unable to answer for thirty-six years, Dr. Z offered his delicate assessment with a slight upward inflection at the end: "So, it seems like you're thinking 'no'?"

That sounded exceptionally definitive to a chronically indecisive person.

"No, no…I wouldn't say that. I'm not ready to say 'no.' " Despite his best—and incredibly gentle and thoughtful—attempts to help me land on an answer once and for all, I still didn't know if I wanted to a have a child.

How could I say never to motherhood when I don't know how I might change and mature over the coming years? What if, when I'm all grown up (say, when I'm fifty-seven or so) I realize that I in fact do want a child? *Holy crap! I want a child, but biology has closed that door, and my younger self should've known better.* It's daunting to make a final decision about the rest of my life with that timer running. Five years of consideration can feel bizarrely like five minutes when you know that when the buzzer dings, you can never reset it. *Decide now to change your life forever, flip your marriage on its head, create another life whose life—and those of the people she touches—will forever be affected by you.* I just can't. It's too many "nevers" and "forevers." But when I admit, *I can't…* the pit in my stomach, the tug in my throat, the anxiety that feels like it may only be alleviated by the angels themselves sending me a signed and sealed letter confirming that I've made the right decision…

To think that I might one day be a mom is easy. There's nothing scary about that: you love your life now and are able to imagine you might also someday love your life with a child and have this whole other kind of existence with a whole new purpose; you'll suddenly be really important, to the child directly and to the world indirectly, because you're charged with the task of raising her. I don't want to be *that* important now…but what if I never am? What if I'm missing out on some fundamental experience and all my mother-type qualities—which I actually have a lot of—will go to waste? I'm also scared that I might get old in spirit faster without a child to remind me about all those things only kids can see and do. I'll forget the magic. I can already feel myself forgetting. I look at pictures of me as a little girl and I have no memory of what she was thinking, but I bet it was fascinating. I look at her and I miss her. I want to sit down to talk with her and remember, to give her the advice, support, and wisdom only I know to give…

or maybe, I want the advice, support, and wisdom that she could re-give to me. The older I get, the more distant I become from that enchanting little girl, and maybe my own daughter would be a bridge back. *Without that bridge, what if there's no way to reach who I once was before the world tamed me?*

We make decisions all the time about who we invite into our lives; some are much harder to undo if or when those relationships no longer serve us, but they can be undone, or transformed. The only truly permanent relationship decision—"permanent" and "decision" being two words that make me wince when put together—is that of a parent and child. For me, that decision had been postponed for all of my childbearing years up until age thirty-six because of choices and circumstances—some exciting, beautiful twists as well as some frightening, unexpected turns. At twenty-six, I'd found myself beginning to consider divorce from the man I'd held up as ideal since I was seventeen. He was (and is) a truly good kind man who would have made a good kind father, and having children was vaguely in our distant plans in the five years we were together. But—not especially shocking—the partner I deemed perfect in my late teens and early twenties didn't turn out to be perfect for me. Any thoughts of permanence, security, or children vanished as I muddled my way through the experience of being single for the first time in my twenties, with one especially distracting rebound relationship (a polite term for what was really a reckless, misguided infatuation) that left me feeling especially lost.

Amidst all the fumbling and muddling, I met and befriended an exotic (in the sense that he lived in Oklahoma and not Houston) professor/musician/poet. Our friendship delicately evolved into more, an evolution that may have had something to do with Nathan reading poetry he'd written, sometimes with a line or two about me, over the phone while I would soak in a bubble bath in my Houston apartment. It wasn't ideal that he was fourteen years older, and it wasn't ideal that he had an eleven-year-old daughter…I'd simply never imagined myself as a step-parent. Despite, or because of, how immensely Nathan loved Sierra, nine years as a divorced parent had wreaked havoc on his heart and soul—his time with her was limited, and it killed him not to experience all of his daughter's life-moments and days.

On one of his visits to Houston, we were enjoying a meal at my neighborhood pub, Stag's Head. Over a Ploughman's Lunch and glasses of wine, I casually asked if he wanted to have more children. He was gentle but firm: no. He explained he could never risk going through the pain again—the pain of having a child but not getting to raise him or her fully. As he explained, I remember thinking and feeling little more than "hm...okay." I knew developing a serious relationship with him, then, meant I probably wouldn't have children. At the time I didn't stew over it much, given that parenting had always been and remained such a faraway notion for me.

I wasn't one of those kids who fantasized about motherhood. I snuggled and loved my stuffed animals. I craved the company of dogs and cats and horses. I never played with human dolls, except to make imaginary stories with my adult-ish Barbies, dreaming of what it would be like to be a grownup, have a house, date and kiss guys, marry, have a job, and do all the other awesome things adults get to do. Taking care of a baby wasn't part of my pretend time, the way it seems to be for many young girls. Now that I was in the middle of all those awesome adult things, I was happy to give this new love a shot whether a baby was going to be part of the package or not.

Two years into a long-distance relationship with Nathan, I'd grown weary of my teaching job at a private high school; literally, I was weary. I just wasn't designed to wake up at 6 a.m. every morning, living on a few hours of sleep and Frappuccinos to get me through my repetition of the fourth lesson plan of the day. I wanted something different, so I was excited and just a little nervous to quit my responsible job with benefits and move to Norman, Oklahoma. The move was followed by a marriage proposal and relatively long engagement given that after one divorce each, I saw reason to proceed with caution. As we built a trusting partnership together, Nathan slowly began to revise the declaration he'd made at that pub. He was enticed by the idea of being a father again and getting to do it right this time, and he didn't want to keep me from being a mother. I was a broken record: I'd probably want a child *someday* but wasn't ready. We'd both learned the harsh lesson that life's grand plans don't always go... well...the way we planned them. It was all of the unknowns, the endless risks and challenges of parenting that caused the most hesitation for both of us. Throughout my twenties, whenever I pictured this family I might one day create, it included two kids about two years apart—a carbon copy of the family I grew up in. But now, the planner in me couldn't see affording two since I was starting over career-wise and marrying a writer and adjunct professor. I didn't love the idea of having an only child with no built-in playmate, as I couldn't imagine my own girlhood without my brother. Ultimately, as my life started looking less and less like the one I'd grown up with, I felt less and less confident I would know how to navigate parenthood.

So years kept passing and the broken record kept spinning; as I approached thirty-five, the age I'd had in mind as the big now-or-never of getting pregnant, Nathan and I decided to move to the Texas Hill Country. I'd always wanted to live in a small town outside of Austin (weirdly specific for an indecisive person—it turns out there are some things I know I want), and was intrigued by the idea of something new, especially now that Sierra was adrift in teenage-ed-ness and rarely finding her way to our shore. Moving away from her was not easy for Nathan though. So once we'd settled in Wimberley, I thought it would be a good idea to go to counseling together, in part to give him an outlet for his fatherly emotions, which I could try to sympathize with all day long but would never be able to empathize with. Our beloved Dr. Z ended up helping us through all sorts of crises, minor and major, over the years. Meanwhile thirty-five came and went, and I still wasn't ready to be a mom. So Nathan and I took the quandary to a counseling session.

Over the period of about a year, when we didn't have some other pressing matter to discuss with Dr. Z, we'd repeat a version of the exchange in those last two minutes of that first session we'd devoted to the issue. Given that my response never changed, I realized I had to accept that not being ready or able to say "yes" meant I am in fact saying "no." I had to make a damn decision. I needed to commit to living with the conclusion: I am choosing not to have a child. I officially have to give up thinking about what I would experience and learn from giving life to another human and being responsible for her life. In order to cope with that conclusion, I needed to consider all the things I'll never to get to say or do, and to celebrate all the things I won't *have to* say or do. I needed to sit with the feeling of being a mom from time to time, to experience it in my imagination, so that I could at last let it go for good. These letters allowed me to do that. They allowed me to create a fantasy daughter in a fantasy world where I could talk with her and then say goodbye to her.

Letters to the daughter I'll never have

To my baby girl,

I don't know if I owe you an apology…or if I owe
myself an apology, or both, or neither…for not
having you. There are times when your dad and I are
walking with Cayenne through the quiet woods in
the Texas hills; or when we snuggle up by a fire at
Christmas time; or when I'm planting veggies in the
garden, sweat pouring down my back and dirt col-
lecting under my nails—Stoney sitting nearby
meowing "hellos" as he gazes at the butterflies
landing and taking off from the flowers—that I am
so sorry I am not bringing you into this beautiful
world. I am sorry I'm not giving you the chance to
feel the sun on your skin. I'm sorry you will never
know the peace of napping next to Cayenne while
she gently snores and flutters with dreams. I'm sorry
you will never walk through the woods with us. I'm
sorry you will never know the satisfaction of planting
seeds that will grow into food you'll harvest and eat.
I'm sorry you won't know the feeling of a first kiss
with someone you're falling for. I'm sorry for myself
that I won't get to witness all of your firsts, or see the
world once again through the eyes of a child, or learn
who you would become. I won't ever know the unconditional love mothers speak of, or the feeling of
watching part of me come into being and grow into a
whole other miracle of a person.

But let me try to explain why I'm willing to give all that up. While I'm sad I'll never know you, I don't feel I *must* know you for my life to be complete. I think motherhood should maybe be reserved for those who feel they *need* to be a mother. To say we are overcrowding our planet would be a gross understatement. We don't all need to procreate just because we can; there's a lot of work to be done and care to be given for the life already here. Also, I love my life the way it is. Your dad and I don't make a lot of money, and we like not having to. We know you wouldn't need much in the way of things to be happy, but you might need care that we can't afford. And you would most certainly need time and ever-so-much attention: time and attention we already give to what we believe to be worthy endeavors. Also, I love sleep. A lot of it. I need nine to ten hours a night to feel rested, and when I'm not rested I don't have much to give of myself. The burning eyes and physical fatigue make it hard to do anything well. We enjoy our freedom, our flexibility to go places and do all sorts of things. Even as I keep saying "we," your dad and I are also very different people who work hard to strive for peace and compromise in our lives, and we have reservations about the added trials and stress of parenting on our relationship.

And…I'm scared. I'm scared the sacrifices so many mothers make naturally wouldn't be as natural to me. I'm scared I would resent your existence just a little for all that your dad and I would have to change, and I would resent myself for never being the best mom I could to you (no matter how hard I would try). I'm scared that despite the best intentions we would have to raise you to become a healthy, content person who would make the world a better place (a tall order, right?), those intentions might be thwarted by all the unpredictables.

So, I'm choosing not to have you. And I will have to go on for the rest of my life knowing that I gave up my chance to create you, teach you, and learn from you. I am giving up my chance to be your mother. And it will always break my heart a little. But life is full of heartbreaking decisions—one more reason maybe you're better off where you are. So…I will never know you. But you are my daughter, and these letters are for you. These are the things I would want to share with you if I did get to know you.

With all my love,
Mommy

To Daddy's Little Girl,

The most important thing for you to know about
your dad is that nobody will ever love you as fiercely.
I've never known a man so emotionally invested in
his child. He is extremely passionate. He can be
passionately excited and in love, and—as our kind
therapist often reminds me is part of the deal—he
can be passionately sad or outraged at what is not fair
or right. He is sensitive, in every sense of the word,
which is both a reason I have wanted to create and
raise you with him, and a reason I don't.

I'll start with the "reason I don't" part. Your dad
feels the joys and pains in this world intensely. He is
in tune to everything around him, whether he wants
to be or not: sounds, sights, body language, energy.
This means he will feel your pain as if it's his own,
and it will hurt him deeply when he can't make it
better. He will lie awake at night worrying about
whether or not this world is safe and good enough
for you—and sometimes, especially if you inherit his
sensitivity, you will realize how much he feels on
your behalf. You may feel weighed down knowing
that he suffers when he can't protect you from everything. Also, because the things we are sensitive to
and about sometimes differ, we may argue about
how to be best for you. Often, he'll be right—like
when he says we should never have the TV on when

you're in my womb or an impressionable infant. But his rightness is likely to annoy me when I'm sitting in silence instead of watching Clinton Kelly share a recipe for a delicious cocktail on *The Chew*.

As far as the *reasons I do*...he will put so much care into the ways in which he can make your life as fulfilling and safe as possible. While he will try to shelter and protect you from too much noise, too many screens, and as much pain as possible; he will also encourage your freedom and try to offer you experiences that will nurture your soul—stillness and quiet, travel and music. He will always be so tenderly kind and gentle with you. It will take something drastic for him to raise his voice at you. I know all of this because I've witnessed him as a father to his now 21-year-old daughter, your sister Sierra. He still shudders and weeps when he recalls the one time when she was in the middle of a toddler tantrum and he grabbed her arm just hard enough to cause some redness when he removed his hand. I've seen the delighted peace in his eyes when she experiences moments of happiness or awe; and I've seen him suffer actual physical pain when she is hurting. He will value your life as the precious and delicate miracle that it is. I know there are two people in the world he would gladly give his life for: Sierra and me.

I'm so happy that, despite some bumps in the road, he also understands his own worth as a son, father, husband, and uniquely creative person. It hasn't always been easy to be him. He often jokes that his older brothers used to say, "Nathan's not like the other children." His ideas and stories and observations were often met with a confused and sometimes sarcastic, "Thanks for sharing, Nathan." He jokes about this but is also quite open about the pain involved in walking the halls of school feeling like he didn't belong, keeping to himself. He has shown me the huge elm tree on the playground of his elementary school where he spent precious hours alone in its limbs rather than roughhousing with other kids. He dreamt of being Tarzan or Indiana Jones and entertained himself by using plant guides to identify species in his neighborhood. He has always been genuinely special. And despite the challenges of adolescence and early adulthood, he believes in who he is and what he does.

He bestows the gift of words—saying what matters—on those of us who take less time and care with words. Your dad writes a poem every day, and he has for twenty years. Literally. Over 7,000 of his poems crowd the shelves of our home in handwritten journals. He used to do it because he wanted to stick with the practice. He does it now because it is a form of meditation. He has so many thoughts, about so many things. And just like he's taken to dry-stacking rocks into walls and art all over our property, slowly placing each rock where it needs to go in order to hold, he is able to put all those thinkally thoughts into well-placed words that make up poems and songs that hold the truth, the truth of this highly complicated human experience that is so difficult, so often, to articulate. His habit not only keeps him sane, but it offers something important to anyone willing to read. I have always loved that your dad is a writer, an artist...even though artists can be famously tough to live with. (Side note: this is *not* a groundless stereotype; think about it when you're dating! You must be prepared for his mood to be ruined by having to fill out any kind of confusing paperwork just as much as you are for a sudden pouring forth of reverence and rapture in the form of tears at the sight of a sunset over the ocean.) He strings words together, he stacks rocks, he draws wonderful little sketches in his journals nobody else is ever likely to see, he plays music, he sings. He creates beauty, even if that beauty is sometimes sad, every day of his life.

He worries that he talks too much. In your younger years I think you'd make a perfect audience for him. You will receive what he has to say with openness. You might not know what he's actually saying, but you'll have plenty of time to listen. You won't always be thinking of what *you* want to say while he's talking, like most of us grownups do. As you get older, he'll become more self-conscious about talking. He won't want to annoy you. But I hope you keep listening. Maybe together you and I can convince him that struggling to silence yourself just makes you feel like you're always about to explode. Nobody wants to feel that way, right? Maybe together, we could finally make your dad feel the love and peace he so deserves.

Nathan came to me at a time in my life when I was sad and scared, and he listened to me talk and talk. He made me laugh and smile, and he lit up something inside of me. For that I will always be grateful to him, and I owe him my ear whenever he needs it. He and I were friends for a while before I fell in love with him. And even though we've had ups and downs, as you will learn every relationship has, I have never fallen out of love with him and we remain great friends. You will witness how much he loves me in the way he always talks to others about me with respect and admiration, the way he looks at me with his eyes reflecting the beauty he perceives, the way he celebrates my accomplishments, and the way he writes me love notes and poems…and you will learn how a man should love a woman.

~Nathan's wife

by Ashley Brown

A letter from your dad:
~ by Nathan Brown

First, I have to take a little time
to play with the Rubik's-Cube-like
impossibility of the task your mom
has set before me and then stepped
back with her hands on her cute hips
as if to say, "…and could you maybe
have that to me by five, six o'clock?"

So just, write a letter to the daughter
you're never going to have. Sure thing,
Babe—I'll just whip that out for you.

So, here is what you'll learn about poets,
my little one, though it appears you won't
actually have to, the dark and metaphysical,
mind-bending wildness—or the proposition
all by itself—was enough to drive me to day-
drinking. And a fearfully and wonderfully
made margarita is my usual go-to for such
extraordinary occasions and circumstances.

And, it'll likely be the thing I go to again,
when the mind-weight of this grave verdict
truly begins to set in. But I'm not there yet.
Because I can match your mom hem for haw
when it comes to the delicate art of indecision.

Which makes me want to go ahead and say,
quickly, just in case it helps you to know:
I want you—I love even the idea of you
so terribly it ties my arteries into knots.

And, I would die for you, were you to
come along and put me in that position.
But, that brings us to the strange thing
about the hard nature of "wanting…"

Wanting a thing does not make, and
has never made, a thing, necessarily,
the best thing for us—or others,
or the world for that matter.

The truth is that wanting
things, and so many of them,
is the very thing that has brought
civilization and the planet it occupies
to the verge of its great destruction.
We've raised so many daughters…
and wanted so many things for them…
our daughters who then wanted daughters
for themselves…daughters that they, in turn,
wanted so many things for…our ecosystem
is finally running out of room and sustenance
for all the many things and the many daughters.

And I may've lost you at this point, I'm afraid.
But, by virtue of the original, heart-wrenching
request set forth by the mom you'll never have,
I suppose I can't lose a thing I'll never have.

Okay... now... even I'm confused...
So confused I'm going to have to go
and make another margarita I think.

But, my God, if you were here, somehow,
I would do everything I could to, somehow,
make all of this a bit clearer for the both of us.

For now, though, if by chance and the stars above,
it matters—which is another thing you'll learn
about poets: they believe it does—

I love you...

like all craziness...
and with red ribbons,
unicorns, and pink bows.

~Dad

On the conditional perfect...

Even with all my years as an English teacher and
editor, I'm at a loss choosing just one right verb
tense for these letters to you. Please forgive the
inconsistencies. Sometimes you exist for me here in
these pages. You *are*. I *will be* this and do that as your
mother. These letters are my opportunity to be your
mom for fleeting imaginary moments. Other times
you are a conditional perfect "would have been."
The metaphorical aptness of the name of this tense is
hard to ignore. You are perfect only in this conditional, un-manifested existence. If your dad and I
could order up all of the just-right conditions of our
life—financial security, a village of family and friends
to help raise you, an ideal school, guaranteed health
and longevity (something we'd need as older
parents)—our decision might be different. If we
could order up the just-right child—one who
wouldn't test our abilities, our stress-threshold, our
limits—our decision might be different. But sometimes the most courageous choices are made when
we see that we can't have it all and must choose, we
have the *freedom* to choose what to sacrifice in order
to live our best lives.

With love that is, will be, and would have been,
Mom

To my screaming bundle of joy,

Back in my twenties, when I was a high school teacher, we took a group of students to an aquarium for a field trip. I was really tired, maybe even hungover. Some children in a younger group nearby squealed with that dreadful sound of excitement only small humans can make, and the squeal echoed throughout the aquarium over to us. I cringed and, without thinking, told my colleague, "There is nothing I hate more than the sound of laughing children"—a quote I'm still famous for today.

While I don't actually hate the sound of laughing children, it is true that my aural sense is ever so delicate. And it seems especially chafed by those unique sounds emitted by children. I've never understood how tiny people can create such god-awful sounds. These sounds seem to be an inevitable part of the baby package. A part I don't want. Of course when you cry out in pain, hunger, fear, or exhaust-tion, I will want so desperately to soothe you, to make you happy and comfortable. And I know sometimes I will succeed. The beet-red color and heat will slowly leave your face, soaked wet with tears that I will dry, and you'll return to a peaceful little peanut, quietly cooing and mumbling. Other times there will be nothing I can do to help, to make it better. It's these times that just might drive me out of my mind. The combination of the earsplitting noise and the pain it signals is just too much.

Other times, you won't be upset at all. Rather, you'll be filled to the brim with utter delight and excitement to that point when you have to let some of it out, and you'll shriek in a pitch and intensity that is just not natural. I can understand why human babies have the ability to cry loudly. That makes evolutionary sense. For survival, you have to be able to get the attention of those who can help you. But the shriek of joy? There is, simply, no reason for it.

~Your over-sensitive mom

Dear Little Dumplin,

To this day, my mom calls me "Little Dumplin." The names we use for each other seem like an oddly important thing in a family. Or maybe it's not so odd, in that what we call the people we know and love is inextricably tied up in their identity and relationship to us. I always called my parents Mom and Dad, never Mommy or Daddy. I called my grandparents by their first names: Viv (Vivian) and Barbie, Bill and Max (Maxine). We did call Max "Grammy" when we were really little, but it didn't stick. Perhaps my brother Parker and I fancied ourselves too mature for babyish names once we could say all the real names.

We need to decide what you would call your grandparents. Neither of my parents would like anything overly silly. I think my mom Sandra would be happy with "Sandy," a name that evokes her younger years, and my dad Chip has a fun and simple enough name as it is. Your dad's parents would be "Grandma" and "Grandpa" to you, as that's what they've been to all of your cousins. So, your grandparents are Sandy, Chip, Grandma, and Grandpa.

But then, there are those names we just come up with for each other along the way. Growing up I had no special nicknames for my brother, but now I call him Parky—about as creative as I get—even though he's forty-one. He, on the other hand, has always had a unique talent for doling out names for friends and family, some with reasons only known to him. I can't even begin to remember all the pet names I've had, although "Little Ocean Spray" stands out. The one that stuck into adult years is "Little Smooth" or more often just "LS." (I'm seeing a pattern with the *little* thing; I guess that makes sense since "I Am the Little Sister," as my favorite sweatshirt at age three proudly proclaimed). When I was a baby I had chubby, soft cheeks that Parker loved to squeeze, which started a weird cheek obsession in him. Over the years, he tortured me with his constant cheek grabs, sneaking a squeeze or a fly-by brushing if that's all he could get away with. As we grew up, I apparently retained smooth cheeks, although not so chubby anymore. So, Little Smooth I was and am.

Among my mom's many names for me were "Tootles" and a variation "Turtles," inspired by one of my favorite books as a little girl: *Tootles from Tootletown*. She and I just got a kick out of the sound of the word. "Little Dumplin" came about with some help from my stepdad Jack. He's also dubbed Parker "Baby Jesus." Anyway, all of these names are really about love and familiarity. I have often wondered what your name would be. But perhaps more interesting than what we would name you are all the loving things we would call you as we learn who you are.

~Turtles

On your first birthday,

I imagine *my* experience of the first year of your life has been the mother (pun intended) of all roller-coasters. I've been lucky enough to know many parents, including my own mom, who are candid about the fact that suddenly having an infant is not all hearts and rainbows in a magical and wonderful new world us non-parents will never understand. Many mothers admit it can be riddled with depress-sion, resentment, self-doubt and guilt, marital stress, and exhaustion. Of course a lot of that yucky stuff is an inevitable result of learning what it's like to love another more than anyone thought they could, of wanting more than anything to be a good parent and do everything right.

Regardless of what kind of parent I've been able to be for and to you, I have some wishes to share with you on this anniversary of your birth. I hope you have felt safe as you've learned to crawl through your little world, a world that's about to become much bigger. I hope you have enjoyed the feel of super soft blankets on your skin; the sounds of music, laughter, and birds; and the tastes of a cor-nucopia of yummy mushy foods. I hope you have giggled more than you've cried. I'm sure there have been moments when you were a little scared or unsure, but I hope you learned Dad and I will always

be there to try our best to make it—fears, life—
better.

I know the shape and structure of my life will be
drastically different after a year of motherhood: far
fewer jaunts into Austin for coffee with Sarah, or
yoga with Robert, or a show at The Gallery while
Kellie keeps my wineglass full. Despite my best
attempts to avoid getting sucked into the social
world of mommyhood—where there's always a
danger of conversation steering towards kids, part-
ners, and/or parenting—I'll probably have new
mom-friends here in Wimberley. As much as our
world will have changed, I hope Dad and I have
stayed healthy and sane, partly by continuing to do
the things we love and carving out alone time. With
no family in the immediate vicinity to help with
babysitting, though, you'll continue to be with one or
both of us most of the time, so we'll also bring you
along on any activity where there's not a danger that
an outburst you may have will disrupt random un-
suspecting strangers…or friends who quite happily
do not have kids. We'll take you on walks and hikes
and any place without walls or echoes. I'll make you
baby foods from scratch, and I'll keep cooking
delicious grown-up dinners for Dad and me. We'll
spend countless hours out back, with our sentinel
Cayenne looking over you while I tend to the
gardens or work on a piece of furniture. I'll find

some way to incorporate you into my yoga practices (hey, if they can do it with goats…). You'll play on the floor in the library while Dad writes and plays guitar. And yes, sweet darling, I think even you know how hilariously picture-perfect these notions are. You will just as likely cry until you get to watch cartoons most afternoons while I will be lucky if I brush my teeth, let alone make delicious organic meals for all of us. But I can dream.

I know I will have thought about you every minute of every day…wondering if you're happy, wondering if I'm doing the right things for you, wondering, worrying, wondering, worrying. I hope I've made you feel absolutely loved, and I hope we've instilled a baby-level of independence in you so that you can start to navigate this world with confidence.

I'll also wonder: What was it like for you as our faces and voices became more than fuzzy shapes and abstract sounds? What goes through your head while we jog through the neighborhood together and you take in the trees, deer, and people as they whiz by your stroller? Do you have thoughts about these things, or do you simply see them? Do people and animals show up in your baby dreams in weird ways? Do you already know what you like and don't like? What a mystery you will have been to me in your first year. And now, you're really going to start becoming a person, with all of your own ideas and traits and tastes. As you begin the lifelong journey of learning who you are, I will watch in amazement.

Happy birthday, little one!

~Mom

by Norma Brown

About my salad days…

When I was very young, Chip surprised us one
evening by bringing home a Siberian Husky puppy.
He might as well have shown up with a unicorn as
happy as this made me. Sandy was none too pleased,
but I think she knew I'd never get over it if we
weren't allowed to keep the adorable pup, so she
named her Misha. The immeasurable love of a five-
year-old and our six-foot fence with rickety gates,
though, were not enough to contain Misha's instinct
to roam, and she got lost—often, and once for good.
I took it so hard I wept at bedtime each night and
slept with a photo of us together framed in a plastic
heart under my pillow for years (literally). I created a
fantasy scenario that I'd play over and over in my
head of the glorious day she would come running
down the street back home while I was playing in the
front yard. Everything would move in slow motion,
accompanied by a beautiful orchestral soundtrack or
maybe even angels singing, as she bounded toward
me, and we'd embrace in a pile of laughter, tears, and
licks. I honestly don't remember anything about
Misha now, but I remember the love and longing. I
remember the *feelings* of comfort and happiness in the
presence of animals, and I remember my difficulty
healing from the sadness of bonds broken and plans,

especially to do with family (pets included) gone awry.

Some children's first "course" in the meal of life is unbelievably burdened by the harsh realities of their surroundings, family, or situation; they never even get to enjoy that youthful bliss and innocence all little ones deserve for as long as possible. I am profoundly aware and grateful that my first course was a deliciously colorful and nutritious salad, so scrumptious in fact that the loss of our dog was the first—and only for quite some time—major heartbreak in a gentle transition to the next course.

The ingredients of that salad (i.e. idyllic childhood if you're not following along with your dorky mom's attempt at analogy) included well-adjusted parents who loved each other and cherished and supported me and Parker; a sprawling but cozy ranch style house, with a huge yard and pool, on a quiet street in the Houston suburbs; friends who remain friends to this day; comfort and security. Chip worked normal hours running various companies over the years and Sandy stayed home. Parker and I played outside all the time creating games and adventures, safely and freely roaming the neighborhood. From our home we could walk to the bayou, or the Houston Racquet

Club where we had a family membership, or school...though we never did because Mom dropped us off and picked us up every day until we could drive. The only interruptions to my pleasurable and peaceful girlhood were sibling spats—when I lost patience with Parker unfairly winning one of our games, or picking on me solely for his amusement—and the occasional battle of wills among the family. All four of us had strong opinions and tastes and not many qualms about sharing them, sometimes loudly. Parker and I were active in sports, and we were able and encouraged to try just about any activity we wanted: gymnastics, baseball, piano and guitar lessons, horseback riding. Chip and Sandy fostered our interests without ever forcing us into something we didn't want to do (despite Sandy's inner disappointment I was not becoming the ballet dancer she'd hoped for). Chip and Sandy sometimes took a vacation alone, leaving us in the care of one set of grandparents or the other, and they sometimes went out with friends on a weekend night, but family and togetherness were obviously and absolutely their priority. We had a condo in Vail and a lake house in Walden, a short drive from Houston, and we went to both often. We skied and sailed. We went for bike rides and walks. I know...yawn. Nobody ever said salad was exotic.

Inevitably though, even with a caring family and the blessings of a safe cushy life, all children endure some upsets and harms that begin to slowly chip away at our innocence. Outside of losing my unicorn (okay, Siberian Husky), it was sometimes tough being the most frail of the family, especially during our travels. I suffered severe and alarming allergic reactions to the sun while skiing that resulted in more than one trip to the ER and pitiful vacation photos in which my swollen face and red eyes stand out among the three other smiling faces. I came down with strep throat and stomach viruses with peculiar frequency. I became an expert at sleeping with my head down on restaurant tables or curled up in a booth at long dinners out that the other three enjoyed. And my family's reaction to all these fragilities? On one vacation in Vail, they bought me a pin. I loved to collect pins, so this was a treat! It was a simple black square with white words on it. I was just learning to read (and couldn't yet), so they told me it said "World's Greatest Reader." I proudly attached it to my tiny denim jacket among my other treasured pins. I'm not sure when or how I realized that the pin actually proclaimed "World's Greatest Burden." They all thought their prank was hysterical. I join them in laughing about it now, but your sweet dad (and our therapist) suspects it probably wasn't so funny to me then. It's true that I didn't want to be burdensome to the very people my world was made up of. I couldn't help my delicate nature or the fact that my sensitive body and soul sometimes had a hard time with all the stimuli out there. So being thought of as a burden by my family—even in love or jest—probably played a small role in the gradual loss of confidence in safety and consequential building up of defenses we all experience.

Again, I consider myself blessed in that my major traumas as a youngster were being my family's greatest burden despite my best intentions and mourning our lost Misha. Maybe because my childhood was generally smooth sailing, back then I just assumed growing up meant nothing other than creating a reiteration of that life.

Now that I am grown, though, it turns out I'd rather sit with my purring cat Stoney in my lap while he makes happy biscuits, kneading his claws into my thigh, than to hold a human baby. It's hard enough to try to protect my animal "children" from pain or danger, but it's almost do-able, at least. Even with the minimal damage done to me, in an insular life free from malice or hardship, I hurt for that fragile little "World's Greatest Burden" who cried for her dog and whose skin withered under the very sun she loved. I'm not sure I'm tough enough to witness the loss of innocence in my own little girl, knowing I can't protect you from it.

~From one little girl to another

About Grandma and Grandpa...

I would so want you to know your dad's parents, but
because of their ages, I don't know how much time
you would realistically have with them. That thought
is deeply sad for your dad and me. They were such
an integral part of raising your sister Sierra with him.
They have been Nathan's rock: the epitome of
supportive, loving parents. They are truly and simply
wonderful people.

Grandma would have so much to teach you about
beauty, art, patience, and love...and I don't mean
"love" in the general, sometimes meaningless
sense—she really knows how to *do* love in the way
she asks questions about things that matter; in the
way she makes sure homemade breads and deviled
eggs are always waiting for family members when
they arrive and that "healthy" oatmeal cookies are
sent with them when they go; in the way she sends
hand-painted notes for every occasion. She's spent
her life seeing the art in every person, object, animal,
and vista and making beautiful Impressionistic
paintings out of it all.

She is a petite person who moves through the
world slowly and with aching joints. But she is
passionate, vivacious, and strong. She gets tears in
her eyes when she sees news footage of people
suffering due to the latest natural disaster or violent

act. She used to drive herself all over England on solo painting trips. She raised three boys, and somehow maintained her sanity. She played the part of the polite and proper Baptist preacher's wife so well, and genuinely, for most of her adult life, while maintaining her independence and spirit as a shy, sarcastic, smart, insightful, honest, and surprisingly liberal woman.

We immediately hit it off that first time I drove to Oklahoma from Houston to visit your dad and "meet the parents." She had arranged for a house-keeper to clean Nathan's house before my arrival, and she bought him new towels that were arranged neatly in the bathroom. When we arrived at their house, five minutes away from his, I was welcomed with a delicate hug and a glass of Chardonnay. I quickly learned Grandma has a great appreciation for the good things in life. We have bonded over the creation of lovely celebrations whenever possible through the years. It doesn't take much to find an excuse, and out come the cheeses, olives, breads, dips, wine, and candles, all beautifully displayed. Once we clink our glasses and look each other in the eyes for a toast, we fill our plates and sit for mean-ingful conversation (sometimes just us, sometimes with Nathan and Grandpa and even Sierra). I would gladly leave you with her for hours or days on end, knowing that every word that passed between you would be valuable to your growth and your soul. She's not only accepting, kind, and funny…but she's a gifted listener. And little girls need as many listeners as they can get.

But oh how she worries. To her credit, she tries hard not to burden others with her concerns. I imagine her spending early morning hours in her dark, cozy, shag-carpeted art studio in their home, sorting through all of her worries while sipping tea: Will Nathan ever feel proud of himself like he should? Will all of her children and grandchildren be okay, in the end? Will global warming, or our current president, destroy our planet? Will we have enough money to replace our breaking washing machine? Will we *really* like the portrait she painstakingly painted of Cayenne? Are cell phones giving us all cancer? Does she call her children often enough or too often? We wish she didn't worry so much, but it's also something special to know there is someone out there who is always thinking about you, always wanting the best for you. I have been so lucky to have her as a mother-in-law, and who she is makes the decision not to have you even harder, because you would have some of her in you.

Grandpa is equally delightful. He is wise, calm, and patient. In talking with him you will need to learn patience too, because he's going to take his time and choose his words carefully. He was a

Baptist preacher before I knew him, but not your typical Southern Baptist. At some point, you'll learn about the kinds of limitations, judgments, and restraints that often come along with the Baptist religion. He doesn't fit any of the stereotypes. He is open-minded and seems to love all beings because he sees them all as creations of God, as part of God. With great admiration, I witnessed this straight arrow of a man (who won't even take ibuprofen) love and support your sister throughout her teenage rebellions and experimentations, tattoos and piercings, and general alternative-ness...never once doling out judgment. He only sees a beautiful soul who sings like an angel and has always carried wisdom beyond her years. So Sierra knows he is a safe place for her. She looks to both of her grandparents as individual role models and a model of marriage.

Grandpa is unassuming and soft-spoken. Yet he manages to find the most clever times and ways to share bits of the wisdom he has gained in his eighty-five years of life. These days he spends much of his time reading voraciously in his maroon recliner, with about ten books stacked beside him at any given time. But his long and full life began in Cyril, Oklahoma, where he'll tell you he had no idea his family was "poor" despite the fact that he had to sleep on a porch that often let the snow in. He married Grandma sixty-two years ago, and while working as a beloved preacher and raising their boys, he remained a faithful and conscientious partner and husband. It seems to me that as he goes through life calmly and thoughtfully observing it all, he has also remained open to constantly learning and growing... a trait that is sadly rare in a man, a trait he seems to have passed along to Nathan. When I asked him what the secret was to such a long happy marriage, he said the main thing is to always care about your partner's best interests as much as your own. Through all the ups and downs of his personal life; all the highs and lows in the lives of his children, grandchildren, and great-grandchildren; and all the tragedies he and Grandma see covered on the evening World News, he maintains his steady faith in a God that courses through the veins of us all. You couldn't ask for better grandparents.

~Norma and Lavonn's Grateful Daughter-in-Law

A letter from Grandma:
~ by Norma Brown

Wishes for the granddaughter I'll never have...

That you will have a strong and healthy self-esteem to follow your own unique personality and contribution to the world.

That you will know the things in life that are truly important and not just material possessions, fame or fortune.

That you would know the spirit and soul of life as well as the physical and have a strong inner core.

That you might appreciate solitude as well as meaningful personal relationships.

That we could have some meaningful hours together painting in my studio, walking in the woods, by a stream or by the sea—
watching the birds, rabbits, squirrels and flowers in our back garden, coloring Easter eggs together in my kitchen, making cookies to take someone who needs a friend, watching you sing and play a guitar or piano, reading books together.

I wish that I could watch you grow into the beautiful young woman I know you would be—inside and out.

A letter from Grandpa:

~ by Lavonn Brown

Dear "Little One" Number Two—I called my first granddaughter Little One,

Welcome to the world where I have spent over 80 years.

The way you see the world makes all the difference. Obviously we do not all see the world the same. Some see their world as hostile or unfriendly, where everyone is "out to get you." They tend to live with distrust and develop a bunker mentality.

All too many see the world as indifferent or uncaring. They develop a posture of defense and live cautiously.

Others see their world as friendly, gracious, and generous. They develop trust, the ability to love and to be present to the moment. I welcome you to this world.

Your parents will have unbelievable love for you. They will provide everything essential to happiness and trust. They will desire only what is best for you. Welcome to our friendly world.

Your Grandfather

About my parents...

Telling you about my own parents, knowing they will never know you, is even more difficult. They have never pressured me to have children, and they're realistic and understanding of the reasons not to. Sandy once told me she wasn't sure she would recommend the stress of parenting, but that it would be the only unconditional love I'd ever know. She has saved my most precious baby clothes for you. Long ago she bought you a tiny gold ring she'll never get to give you. Occasionally she texts me pictures of adorable baby things she comes across at a store along with a crying emoji. Just as I didn't desperately want children but still have strong emotions about not being a parent, Sandy was never one of those moms tapping her foot waiting for a grandchild... but upon realizing the certainty that she will never have one, she has had some sadness to cope with. She and Chip both appreciate my decision—one it looks like my brother is making as well—but they also have to grieve the lost opportunity to be grandparents. Before I tell you about Chip and Sandy, though, I need to back up to when I was eight years old.

In our house growing up, very little actual living was done in "the living room" with its yellow carpeting, overly firm sofa with an overly loud floral design, and secretary desk covered in fancy knick-knacks. It was reserved for practicing the piano and, for whatever reason, Easter morning egg-hunting and counting. The den was where we all hung out, watched TV, played games, sat by the fire, put up the Christmas tree, and "lived." So when my parents called my brother and me into the living room one Friday evening, we knew something was up. (Looking back, I realize the timing of the start of the weekend was well-thought-out as it gave us two days to gather ourselves before going to school.) They told us they were separating.

I wouldn't be surprised if the sound of my heart shattering was actually audible. As all four of us cried together, my mom and dad assured us it had nothing to do with us and that we would always be a family. In my adult years, I've learned more about their relationship. But all I knew then was they had "differences" and they were separating but not divorcing, meaning they held out some hope of working it out. They did get back together for four years while I went through high school but divorced when I left for college. Chip and Sandy continued to treat each other with kindness and respect, and they were always there for us in ways big and small. But still, their separation just plain sucked. They each remarried when I was in my twenties. Admittedly, I wasn't thrilled initially by the additional change caused by bringing stepparents into the mix of our family. Mom will never let me forget a proclamation I apparently made about a particular occasion we were planning: "I don't want to share it with random stepparents!" (She thinks it's just another hilarious Ashley saying.) The silver lining to my parents remarrying is that I wanted them to be happy and they are. I have caring and sweet stepparents I've grown to consider much less "random." I love them both, along with my two very cool stepsisters who are dear friends. We're all okay. But the fact that my parents are not together—that they wouldn't be grand-parenting you together—is another hitch in my parenting game plan. I don't blame them or have any resentment about it. It's just the village it takes to raise a child would be all spread out in different homes with "steps" and complications. Nonetheless, I love my mom and dad so much, and I'm sorry they will never know you.

Love,
Mom

I always thought it would be interesting if you had a daughter and she was a throwback to someone more like me, which would be highly amusing to me.

~ Sandy

About Sandy...

Sandy grew up in the small town of Lake Jackson, Texas. She was the oldest child with three brothers. Her dad Viv, born and raised in South Africa, was a smart, kindhearted man, who worked hard—as a professor at Texas A&M and Director of Agricultural Research at Dow Chemical—to take care of his family. Her mom Barbie was a good woman, but she struggled with depression, often turning to alcohol to self-medicate, the source of some family tension and embarrassment. She also worked hard to meet the demands of raising four children with modest means, but while Sandy knew her parents loved her, she also knew her mom wasn't a very happy person. And she was such a sensitive little girl that she often threw up in the mornings before school, a physical manifestation of the friction and anxiety she perceived in their household.

Perhaps because it was a different time (growing up in the 1940's), she wasn't exactly showered with affection or nurturing guidance. She explains parents back then just didn't "spoil" their children like they do now; they were supportive and caring, but Sandy—as the oldest—was expected to handle a lot on her own. And she did quite well, excelling in school, learning to sew her own clothes, and taking good care of her youngest brother when her mom was busy. Her dad had always wished to be able to provide the best education for her, but they were only able to afford two years at Texas Women's University. So as a young adult, she moved to Houston and became a secretary.

Sandy is stronger and more selfless than I understood growing up (after all, we don't often have the perspective to analyze our parents or give them their due credit when we're small). Even though she didn't have the best model, she figured out the mothering thing pretty darn well, and has always made me feel not only loved but secure. It would be naïve to think she didn't have times of sadness or stress, but I was largely shielded from any of that, allowing me to experience a childhood free from the burden she had felt as a girl. I felt surrounded by happiness for the most part, and she was present with us. Although, we do laugh today about the fact that she hired night nurses and nannies to help with my brother and me, despite not working and having no real reason to need such help; she just thought that's what you did if you could afford it. She was doing her best to be a mom and wife with the tools she had, even if some of the tools handed down to her weren't the sharpest. What I admire most about her is that she was, and still is, willing to learn.

She created so many simple yet lovely moments for me of the sort that were likely never created for her. She set up picnics on quilts in our yard. She played "I Spy" with me after school from the wooden bench on our front porch. Every Easter, she would cleverly create what looked to be large dusty paw prints on the ground going from the sidewalk into our home...leaving no doubt in our little minds the magical bunny had visited us. She rocked and sang me to sleep even when I was way too big and old to be rocked. She made me hot chocolate with marshmallows on cold days. She tucked me in every single night, telling the monsters to go away, until I decided I was too big and didn't need tucking in anymore (which, let's admit, was probably well into my teens).

She also accepted who I was despite her dashed hopes and expectations of what her daughter would be like. She had dreamed I would be a little ballerina who loved hearts and pink, jewelry and dresses. Instead, she got a tomboy who wanted to wear her brother's clothes and play football. I took my tomboyishness very seriously. Because she let me have the short haircut I wanted, I was often mistaken for a boy out in public, and I didn't mind. If it bothered her, she never showed it. She never forced me to take a dance class or wear froofy dresses. She did decorate my room with hearts, but I didn't really mind that—it was a happy, comfy room.

With her sense of humor, she would be thrilled if you turned out to be the feminine and graceful mini-Sandy she always wanted, thus dashing my own hopes of having a mini-me! I would, of course, let you wear pink dresses and take dance classes and indulge any interest you have. But I also admit it would be hard to have a girly girl rather than a cute sporty tomboy.

Sandy is creative and loves to draw, one thing she did pass on to me (she's much better though). She knows all the practical stuff a mom should, like how to mend clothes, get stains out, iron shirts, polish silver, and wrap a gift perfectly. As many times as she's tried to teach me these skills, I'm afraid they just don't stick. So you'd have to learn those things directly from her.

While it'd be hard to ask for a better mom, every mother and daughter clash, and parents can't always be just what their kids want or need in every moment. As a tiny person, I remember squeezing her hand tighter around my own, as we would walk through a store, because I wanted to feel like she really *wanted* to hold my hand. I craved that overt affection that just wasn't the norm in families when she was growing up. She didn't always control her temper, and sometimes she would yell when I accidentally spilled or broke something. I used to swear to myself I'd never do that with my child (a promise I'm not sure I could keep). These minor transgressions are easily forgivable though.

In my teenage years, I'm not sure it was as easy, as we began to get on each other's nerves regularly. That's when I think it was most difficult for her that I didn't want the same things she deemed important, things she didn't get to have or be growing up in a small town. She wanted me to be a joiner, specifically of all the private-school types of things: country club style shows and debutante parties. She desperately wanted me to join a sorority in college. That sounded like hell to me—I never understood the concept of paying for a group of people to accept you into their "sisterhood," if you met their standards, so you could all dress alike and party together. Anyway, Sandy and I argued a lot. But I could never stay mad at her. Even after a screaming match, slammed doors, and a few hours of giving her the silent treatment, I would still end up snuggling next to her in her fuzzy pink robe late at night when I needed a break from homework. The arguments abated when I went to college and we no longer lived under the same roof...except when I called home to tell her I'd gotten my eyebrow pierced.

Sandy was diagnosed with breast cancer when I was twenty-three. She underwent a double mastectomy and years of complications due to a compromised immune system. She's also lost two close friends to cancer. It seems like these challenges, along with all the other experiences that tend to add to our wisdom as we age, have opened her mind and heart and given her a deeper perspective. She is a more spiritual person than she used to be, open to practicing self-healing and positive thinking techniques. We can still drive each other crazy with our differences from time to time. (Even though she loves Nathan, and knows he's a good husband, I think it just about killed her I had no interest in finding a wealthy businessman to marry. Boring, right?! And it's best if we don't talk about politics). But...I genuinely enjoy her company. We email each other almost every day, sometimes five or ten times. We love having dinner together, especially if martinis are involved, and talking about the past, the future, relationships, the occasional gossip, and how to handle life's curveballs and pains with peace of mind. Sandy is one of few people in this world I never have to pretend around, because she's not only my friend but my mom, and I don't care if she doesn't like everything about me. I know she loves me and

cherishes my existence. And I think she would make
a wonderful grandmother.

Love,
Sandy's daughter

by "Sandy" Harrington

A letter from Sandy to me:

~While Sandy knew I was working on these letters to you, she decided to write one to the daughter she does have. I'd like to share it with you.~

My sweet daughter,

I'll never forget the moment, 39 years ago. Viv had stopped by to visit and the phone rang. I was in the study and it was my OB/GYN's office calling to say I was going to have a girl. I was totally suffused with joy! I never realized until that moment how much I wanted a girl. Our family had so many boys on both sides (all your cousins, except Laura, my three brothers, Dad's three brothers) and it never occurred to me that I would have anything but a second boy. I couldn't keep it to myself and told Viv, telling him it was not to be shared. Of course, he immediately went back to Lake Jackson and told Barbie.

I had a wonderful time decorating the nursery and ordering a pink gingham crib pillow with "Ashley" embroidered on it. Your name was my third choice—I had always loved Amanda, but the cat got that as I never dreamed I'd have a daughter to give it to. The second was Lauren, but Gary already had a Laura, so that was out. As it turns out, you were the perfect Ashley. What a beautiful and easy baby you were! A total joy—always happy and easygoing, and so, so cuddly. How I loved hugging you while singing "You Are My Sunshine" at "tuck-in" time. You did balk at the large hair bows I tried to get you to wear, and you did balk at ballet lessons. But you patiently endured the years of eyelet lace, bubblegum pink walls, Laura Ashley prints and ribbons in your bedroom. It was inevitable that you eventually took a stand and insisted on beige walls covered with Garth Brooks posters.

You've remained the joy of my life, and I couldn't ask for a daughter I'm more proud of. You became your own person and have accomplished so much. I admire your independence and abilities and talents.

You will always be my sunshine.

All my love,
Your Mom

About Chip...

Chip had a pretty idealistic upbringing in Houston. If you ask him about his childhood, it's not likely he'll mention a single problem. His parents didn't have much money, but they were very loving and involved. Chip had three younger brothers who all got along, great friends, and a superb private school education due to a scholarship. He was the all-American good kid, captain of the football team and class president who went on to attend Yale where he was a member of the infamous and exclusive Skull and Bones society, going to parties with the likes of George W. Bush—who would one day become President of the United States—and thriving on the debate team with John Kerry, who would go on to one day challenge George "Dubya" for that presidency.

Chip was pretty close to a perfect father in the eyes of a little person. He worked 9-5 every day of the week, as an entrepreneur and CEO of various companies, and he always seemed to love his work. I think that's so important and part of why he was able to be such an energetic father to us. He never seemed worn down or too stressed to enjoy life. Parker and I used to wait for him at the end of our street to come home from work. He would stop, and one of us (we'd alternate) would hop on his lap in the driver's seat and steer the car the rest of the way home while he operated the break and gas pedals. He played board games with us. He would set up the Slip N' Slide in the backyard and blow up the pool floats. He'd play H-O-R-S-E and P-I-G with us, teaching me the right form to shoot a basket. He coached both of our baseball and softball teams every year, but he was never that overbearing kind of coach or dad. It was so clear we were all just doing these things to have fun.

He loved to sail, and he loved music. He even owned a recording studio for a while, which seemed unbelievably cool to me. Some of my favorite memories of and with him are idyllic Saturdays spent sailing (never mind the obligatory hours of grumbles and work on the boat that seemed to have a problem every time we arrived at the marina), visits to the studio to gawk at all the fascinating equipment, and regular afternoons at home when he would play music. He plays the piano beautifully. To this day, I am always comforted by the sound of a piano. He was also always playing great record albums and making carefully labeled mix tapes. He bought me my first CD player and CD (The Cowboy Junkies). He made Parker and me feel absolutely protected and free to be ourselves. He paid for two private school educations, two college educations, and threw in one grad school education for me. He's bought me all of my cars. So, I'm spoiled, yes. I *feel* loved, though, not spoiled. He mentored me through the failure of my first marriage. And if I'm ever in any kind of trouble, I know he's there.

I suppose it may sound like I've been harder on Sandy than Chip, so I must add the disclaimer, in defense of all moms or whichever parent may be home with the kids most, my dad wasn't the one in charge, the one who said yes or no, and he got space from us every day at work. This freed him from much of the conflict and the harsh judgment of a child. That came a little later for us.

On that evening my parents told us they were separating, Chip picked me up and held me while I sobbed. He was crying too, of course, perhaps because as a grownup he knew what was coming. It was a pivotal time for our relationship. He was still always around for sports games, holidays, and any important event whatsoever. But he wasn't around for the day-to-day, and that was not an easy adjust-ment. He became fun dad, living in a condo where we'd have sleepovers and eat donuts for breakfast. There were times that being with just him and Parker was challenging; they weren't especially understand-ing of my sensitive little girl brain and heart. I would get exhausted playing outside long before they did, and I'm pretty sure the horror movies they liked to watch didn't help with my nightmares.

When my dad moved back in when I was
thirteen, I wasn't having it. I was a moody teenager,
and I didn't want to have to adjust once again. I
didn't want him around every day. I found him
annoying...and for no real reason. (I'm afraid the
annoying factor is an inevitable part of being a parent
at some point in the journey.) I made no effort to
hide my aggravation. I was mean to him, giving him
curt responses to questions and rolling my eyes. I
think it broke his heart, and I only sort of cared.
When I was getting ready to leave for college,
though, we went to a family therapy session where he
choked back tears as he talked about his fear that we
wouldn't keep in touch closely since he and my mom
were getting divorced. His candor and sentiment got
to me. Plus, I was nervous to leave home, and the
scared little girl in me wanted my mom and dad. I
emerged from my stubborn grumpiness and went
back to appreciating the caring father and good
person he was.

While I wouldn't necessarily trust him to feed you
the healthiest snacks or to make sure you don't fall
off something while playing, I do know his love for
you would be boundless. He would have so much
fun with you...playing music, throwing a football,
just chatting. There's something about the idea of my
baby girl in my dad's arms—it feels like that would
be the one gift I could give him to say thank you for

all he's done for me, all he has given me. And I'm sorry for my parents that I am not giving them the gift of you, of being your grandparents.

Love,
Chip's daughter

We have stopped for a moment to encounter each other, to meet, to love, to share. This is a precious moment but it is transient. It is a little parenthesis in eternity. If we share caring, lightheartedness, and love, we will create abundance and joy for each other. And then this moment will be worthwhile.

~ Deepak Chopra

On kindness...

One thing I am proud of is that I am capable of empathy, and have an innate sense of caring for most living beings. "Proud" may not actually be the right word—I'm not sure if we're proud of things we were just born with. It's not like I worked to develop this trait. But it is one I cherish and hope will also be part of you.

When I was little, I imagined that everything had feelings—or at least a spirit of some kind—from rocks and blades of grass to my stuffed animals. I had a collection of over one hundred beloved stuffed critters. I kept them in a big wicker bed that ultimately disappeared under the pile, and I would alternate which four or five I slept with each night so that they would all feel equally loved. Your uncle Parker, who perhaps was not born with the gift of empathy (despite his many others), would sometimes delight in blowing up a toy animal with a firecracker or subjecting it to some other tortuous act. I don't think I fully showed it lest I be mocked, but it always broke my heart.

And even while logic tells me now that *things* can't or don't feel, I still look at rocks and even stuffed animals as if they do. Can it hurt to consider things—in addition to every living creature—with respect and kindness? I think of animals, even the un-real ones, when I think of empathy because it seems that's where it began for me.

Before I go on, I realize as your mom, I should stop and explain what this big word actually means. Empathy means the capacity to really put yourself in the shoes of another…to feel what another is feeling in an effort to understand and connect. It's not sympathy, and it's not pity. It's an awareness of, and caring about, the feelings and experiences of others, as if they were just as important and real as your own. So while I'm a bit ashamed to say that it's actually more challenging to apply these values to humans, what with our unique ability as a species to be stupid and mean, I do try. I try to put myself in the shoes of others, even when I can't know exactly what it feels like to walk in those shoes. If there is anything I can instill in you, if you aren't born with it, I hope it will be the ability to empathize with all that is Other. Because, in the end, there really isn't any

"Other." We're all connected, and when we practice compassion, this great big ball of energy we all belong and contribute to, just maybe, gets brighter.

Love,
Mom

To my little omnivore,

I'm pretty sure I'd be a total freak about what you eat and what you don't, constantly weighing the nutritional and ethical issues that have to do with where our food comes from and how it gets from the source to your little mouth. I'm a pescatarian, and I'd like to explain a little bit about why. Theoretically, I don't want to force my views on you, especially before you're old enough to understand, but if I'm honest, I kind of do.

When I was sixteen, I stumbled across a documentary that vividly portrayed how cows end up as meat. It was about factory farming: two words that really ought not to ever go together. But I'm afraid we live in a world of factories and mass production—yet another reason I'm not sure we need to add to the masses. In this film, I saw images of muddy stockyards full of cows with barely enough room to turn around. I saw calves being forcefully taken from their mothers to be chained for the rest of their short lives before they would become veal. I saw the fear in the eyes of those about to be slaughtered. I couldn't abide any of it. I couldn't stand to think I was complicit in excusing that treatment of living creatures, so I gave up red meat. Keep in mind I was only a teenager, so I didn't quite think through all the other kinds of animals and their plights just yet because I hadn't seen them on TV.

A few years later, I was driving down the freeway on one of my many trips between college in St. Louis and Houston. The smell hit me first. Then, as I drove past the eighteen-wheeler, I saw crates upon crates of live chickens packed so closely together, they were all twisted and smushed. At my eye level, I saw one lying dead among all the others. I had the same nauseating feeling in my gut I'd had a couple years before. Uncontainable tears fell down my cheeks for the next twenty miles. I haven't eaten chicken since, and my heart still sinks into my stomach every time I smell one of those trucks up ahead.

As an adult, I've learned more about where our foods come from, about the difference between factory farms and family-owned organic farms, about the regulations and lack thereof for the care and treatment of animals born and raised to become food for us. I'll *very* occasionally eat meat now if I feel sure that the animals who provided that meat were able to live natural lives, free to be outside and roam and act like cows or deer, until they were quickly and as-humanely-as-possibly killed. While I respect my friends who hunt and eat their prey—using all parts of the animal—I know I don't have it in me to commit the act myself. And if I can't take the life of the animal, I'm just not sure I've earned the right to eat the animal.

All this is to say, what and how to feed you would stress me out, and your dad would be equally concerned. While he's not a vegetarian or pescatarian, he is highly conscientious about where food comes from and what we put in our bodies. Admittedly, I have fed Cayenne chicken her whole life because I know dogs need meat to be healthy, being carnivores and all. While we are omnivores, without a particular need for meat, since I cook meat for my dog I suspect I'll do the same for you unless I learn more about healthy vegetarian diets for children. But whatever I provide for you, I will diligently consider the source, because we are what we eat. And I don't want any part of the cruelty, the pesticides and hormones, of the factory farming process to become some part of you. Then, when we're old enough to talk about it, you can decide what feels right for you, and I will respect it. But you'll have to cook your own pork chops!

~Mom

About those first movies...

I hope the first storybooks you hear and read will stand out more in your memory than movies. Although, my feminism, or cynicism—or whichever -ism is most apt—leads me to be nearly as suspect of certain classic children's books as those traditional animated movies. They can be equally guilty of sending subtle but problematic messages about gender roles, stereotypes, and body image. Perhaps I'm overanalyzing how every book, show, and movie will make their mark on my clean slate of a baby girl. But I can't help it.

It's not totally clear to me how the movies of my early childhood shaped my developing brain, but I'm sure they played a role. I loved sad movies that made me cry, and I preferred movies about animals. The Disney-princess movies didn't interest me. I watched our VHS tape of *Bambi* so many times I knew every line. Most of the story features a young fawn coming of age, making friends and of course falling in love... happy stuff! But the imprint that *Bambi* had on me came mostly from the scene when Bambi's mother is shot after he's gotten all excited about finally getting to go out into "the meadow." It hurt my heart every time—imagining the little guy losing all he'd known about what was safe and right in the world to a heartless hunter. *The Fox and the Hound* was my other early favorite: the story of a fun-loving fox pup, Todd, becoming best friends with a sweet goofy hound dog, Copper. The anguish comes at the end of this one, when we have to accept the grown fox and dog cannot be friends in the human world of hunters and hunted. I tear up just thinking about it.

The stories and tribulations of the human characters in other movies seemed so silly in comparison: Jasmine's struggle to come to terms with the expectations placed on a princess, Beauty's inconvenient attraction to the Beast, Cinderella's unfortunate home life. It's the animals' pain, often at the hands of people, that got to me. Was it the movies that fostered my love for and sensitivity to animals? Or was I drawn to those movies because of something I was born with? It's hard to know. It's also hard to know how they might affect you. If you're like me, your little heart will break for Bambi, Copper, and Todd. Do I really want to expose you to that? Or, what if you watch these movies and don't shed a tear? How will I cope with having a child who doesn't feel the loss of Bambi's mom or of the fox and hound's friendship? Some serious questions here.

~Over-thinking Mom

As long as they roam the earth, people can never harm the pure of heart.

~ Jack

To my little believer,

My parents didn't have many guidelines with regard to what I was allowed to watch, so along with the cartoon movies, some of my early favorites were slightly more mature. For instance, in addition to memorizing *Bambi*, I also knew by heart just about every line of the raunchy Tom Hanks comedy *Bachelor Party*. There are few scenes from that movie I feel comfortable describing for you, but you can guess based on the title. *Legend* is not nearly as salacious and was only rated PG, but it does feature a rather terrifying and very red Satan, or "Lord of Darkness," as a main character that I'm not sure my tiny eyes needed to see. But Tim Curry's eerie portrayal of the Dark Lord isn't what stuck with me...it was the unicorns.

This is a fantastical movie starring a teenage Tom Cruise; it's a love story but mostly a story about good and evil, light and dark. Cruise's character Jack is a pure boy who lives among the animals in nature. He has fallen for Lili, and he wants to show and share with her all that is beautiful, so he takes her to see the last two unicorns on Earth. He explains the unicorns represent and maintain goodness; they preserve the light in the world. Lili of course messes it all up by touching one of the unicorns despite Jack's instructions. All hell breaks loose, literally, when one of the unicorns is wounded by a goblin doing the Dark Lord's work and her horn is cut off. I wish I could describe for you how profoundly this story affected me every time I watched: the beauty of the white unicorns running through a stream when we first see them; the heart-wrenching scene when Jack comes upon the remaining unicorn standing guard over the fallen unicorn, surrounded by white snow, and he bows asking for forgiveness with tears streaming down his cheeks; the light returning to the universe when Jack returns the horn to her.

I *believed* in these unicorns, in their magic, in the light. I felt such anger at Lili for touching one of them. I felt so distressed by the cold darkness that swept over the scenes when the horn was taken, by the sadness inflicted on the pure creatures that before knew "only love and laughter." And, as foolish as it might sound, I have taken that belief in those unicorns with me into adulthood...in the sense that I believe in legends, and angels, and the power of symbols...and in the sense that all I can't see and don't know feels like magic to me. But angels and magic can be tough to talk about in adult company.

Oddly enough, though, unicorns have suddenly become quite popular among kids and adults alike. I think we're feeling scared of the darkness that threatens our country, and our planet. While people may not come right out and say it, we need unicorns just as much as the fantastical characters of *Legend* needed them. I like to believe they're out there, making sure the pure of heart are protected and able to carry their light with them. This is the kind of magic I hope you will believe in.

~Your big believer

On your first day of school,

Another quandary of your early years would be education. I recognize my concerns are ironic in that school for me, all the way from pre-school through 12th grade, was pretty great. It was like a home away from home. Sure, there were tough days and moments of stress, just like in any home, but it was a comfortable, easy place to be. I've come to realize how rare it is for school to feel like a safe place for kids, and how rare it is that schools succeed in teaching what kids should learn: how to use the muscles of their brains, how to communicate well, how to absorb information, how to be compassionate, how to find and foster one's own strengths. I would hope school would nurture a desire to read, talk, write, ask questions, and to work hard; but how many of them really do that?

I attribute some of the warm fuzzies I have about my own education to the fact that my parents sent me to a private prep school (the same one Chip had attended). I'm not sure if it was the exorbitant tuition or the laughable homogeneity of the tiny student body that earned the school its rightful reputation as the snobbiest in Houston. But despite some of the downsides, I felt comfortable in those intimate classes with the individual attention from caring and competent teachers. I was given all sorts of opportunities spanning academics, arts, and sports. I actually learned stuff. It's harder for me to trust the public school system: the larger student bodies where a kid can get lost in the crowd, the poorly paid teachers who are asked to spread themselves so thinly, the emphasis on nonsensical standardized testing. Public or private, my dilemma would be, how can I send you away every weekday of your life for nine months a year to some other place, with all those other people?

Back when I thought I would most likely have a child, I figured I'd choose the homeschooling route in order to protect you from all the risks and down-falls of the school system. In an ideal world, your dad and I would plan an amazing curriculum, that would include foreign travel as a family and learning through experience. You could learn to speak multiple languages and somehow also learn math and science and make lifelong friends. Clearly, the world is not ideal, and there are many problems with the home-schooling plan: A) We wouldn't really know how to follow through with these grandiose ideas, B) It's quite obvious that staying at home all day with your two parents is no way for you to grow up and live and learn, C) I can't imagine parents surviving without those hours when their kids leave the house for a while so they can clean, work, and enjoy some peace and quiet, and finally D) How would I avoid screwing you up myself? Plus, even though social-ization can be a scary part of growing up, it is a necessary part. So of course I'd want you to be out and about with others, finding friends you laugh with, playing, bonding, flirting, competing, joking, deciding what and whom you like.

Most parents seem to accept the good, bad, and ugly of the schooling of their children and deal with it like normal humans. Not me. I can't fathom subjecting you to god-knows-what in all those days away for twelve years, entrusting you and your delicate developing brain to so many unknowns. Nor can I fathom the colossal responsibility of entrusting myself with your delicate development. There's just so much potential to get it wrong, and I would so want to get it right for you. Therefore, you see the problem.

~ Mrs. Mom

About dreams...

I dream so often and so vividly, I wonder if I actually get any rest when I sleep. My "night life" is so exciting that I often wake exhausted at the start of my day life. I'm aware of my dreams throughout the night, and I remember not only the events but also the images and emotions from them well into the next day and beyond. While I experience the occasional ecstasies within my dreamworld, the dreams usually have at least some component of stress, anxiety, sadness, or fright.

The first dream I ever remember having was a nightmare. I was three. I had seen a music video that day. Back then, MTV (Music Television) was a very cool TV channel that played music videos all day. The video was Michael Jackson's "Thriller." I have no recollection of the actual experience of seeing it, and don't remember if I felt particularly scared as the troop of zombies danced along to Jackson's catchy pop hit. Somehow, though, I still remember the dream in striking detail. I was lying in bed, and all those zombies were creeping toward me, coming for me. Of course I awoke right as they reached my bed. Yikes...I hope sharing this doesn't give you your own nightmares.

As a child, I continued to have nightmares along with some pleasant dreams. I even had a few lucid dreams, and when I realized I was actually in a dream, I would immediately try to jump off of something high and fly, but I don't remember it ever working. Maybe since I knew I was dreaming, I was subject to the laws of real life. These days, no matter the sort, I dream and dream and dream; at least it feels that way. The science of it and how many hours a night I'm actually dreaming are unclear to me. I dream about my high school boyfriend I'm no longer in touch with—I'm always thrilled we are close again and desperate for his attention. I dream about being back together with my ex-husband—I panic at some point wondering why we are back together and where Nathan is. I dream about travel: flying, boating, swimming, getting lost in hotels with endless elevators. I dream about total fantasy worlds and Armageddon-type situations. I dream about intimate encounters with people I love, from an old best friend to Garth Brooks. I dream about the mundane, and often during the day I can't recall if some little thing happened in a dream or real life, which gets confusing. Lately, I've dreamed numerous times about being trapped in some kind of close relationship with Donald Trump and feeling horrified but also responsible for somehow keeping him in line. I dream of the cats and Cayenne being in danger or injured, and these are some of the most difficult to get out of my mind.

Sandy tells me she began having nightmares about bad things happening to Parker and me when we were each born, so I can only imagine how your existence would affect my dreams. Sandy and I have other similarities in our dream world that I wonder if you might inherit. For over thirty years we've both had a recurring nightmare of running through the house I grew up in feeling scared, like we are in danger, and not a single light switch works. It's a terrifying, powerless feeling. While the generic underlying symbolism seems obvious, I find it fascinating that my mom and I share a dream that is so exactly the same, right down to the details.

Perhaps my crazy dreamworld is a result of my subconscious sorting out fears and worries and troubling images from my daily life so that I'm more stable in my waking hours. After all, I am impressively stable (wink, wink). Who knows. Whatever dreams are, wherever they come from and whatever purpose they serve, I'll be so curious about yours, and I'll hope they're a little more peaceful than mine so you can at least get a good night's rest.

~Dreamer

"Stoney" by Ashley Brown

The other night dear, as I lay sleeping,
I dreamed I held you in my arms.

My sunshine,

Sandy always rocked me to sleep singing, "You are my sunshine, my only sunshine." I would do the same for you. While I realize Stoney is in fact a cat, I joke with your dad that he's my "baby boy"— something about his needy meows, his insatiable thirst for affection and company, his peaceful purrs when he's snuggled on my lap, his obvious need for me even now that he's grown into an independent smart resourceful little guy. Anyway, I like to sing this same lullaby to him and he seems to quite enjoy it…I've even learned to carry the tune.

There aren't many things I'm sure about when it comes to how to parent or what I would enjoy about parenting, but sharing songs and books tops that short list. One of the first books my mom read to me was *Goodnight Moon.* I still have the copy we used, its spine taped together. How peacefully beautiful it would be to lull you off to sleep with the same book, the same story of the little rabbit saying goodnight to the mice, the mittens and kittens, and the cow jumping over the moon, while the old lady whispers "hush."

When I learned to read, I didn't have much interest in exerting the effort. Sandy quickly realized the way to get me reading was to find any and every book about animals (surprise, surprise). One of the first I read all by myself was *The Velveteen Rabbit*. It's a sweet story about how a little boy's true love for his stuffed rabbit is strong enough to make the toy real. The boy gets sick, though, and all his toys must be taken away. The rabbit gets to go on living a real rabbit life out in the woods, but he doesn't get to snuggle with the boy anymore, and the boy will never know his beloved rabbit is hopping around out there. It's a recurring dichotomy: the story breaks my heart, but it also makes me believe in the magic of love. I still have my own "Rabby," with his de-stuffed head and disintegrating ears. He's been with me for about thirty-five years, and I'm pretty sure he's real. I would love for you to meet him...but I don't think I'd let you snuggle and slobber on him. Don't worry, you'd have your own chosen favorite.

As an adult, I now have another special rabbit. Last Christmas, Sandy gave me one that looks just like the stuffed rabbit of the storybook...velvety soft with floppy ears. She knows how much that book meant to me, to us. Unwrapping and opening her gift made me feel like a giddy kid again. It was so much more fun than opening a box to find a nice sweater. Then she told me she'd spent time with the stuffed animal, infusing it with positive energy and comfort for me, so that if I'm ever sad or scared—even when Mom isn't here anymore—I can hold it close. You see, the magic of love doesn't just exist in stories. I named the rabbit "Sandy." And I *would* happily pass her along to you some day. I hope you would love her truly, believing she is more than a toy.

~Sandy's Daughter

by Ashley Brown

Order is a lovely nymph, the child of Beauty and Wisdom; her attendants are Comfort, Neatness, and Activity; her abode is the valley of happiness: she is always to be found when sought for, and never appears so lovely as when contrasted with her opponent, Disorder.

~ Samuel Johnson

Sweet Pea,

I wonder, will I ask you to make your bed every day? I remember so logically inquiring of my mom over and over why in the world it mattered if we picked up our socks from the den or made our beds every morning just to un-make them every night. For whom were we doing all this work? The only possible explanation could be that she would regularly have impromptu fancy parties in the middle of the day, during which the guests would roam into all of the rooms of the house and judge our neatness.

Of course, that wasn't happening. And she never really had an acceptable explanation for us at the time. It was one of those "just because" kind of things. She's admitted now that she didn't personally care at all if our rooms were neat or tidy—her own parents never made her clean up or do chores. She just figured as a mom and housewife in a nice suburban neighborhood, there were certain things you ought to require of your kids.

Over time, as I grew up and moved into my own places and spaces...I can't pinpoint exactly when it happened... I became a bit of a neat freak. I'm fairly manic about cleaning if company is coming. And when your dad is out of town, I look forward to exciting Saturday nights organizing this and rearranging that. It brings me pleasure to wipe counters, to clear corners of cobwebs, to de-clutter, to find just the right place for belongings and to create spaces that are just that: spaces. It can be tough though to stay on top of Cayenne's hair all over the rugs, dust on the bookshelves, and bathrooms that seem to need cleaning five minutes after I've scrubbed and scrubbed. I can't imagine how much harder it'll be to stay on top of with a little one pitter-pattering all over. Maybe I will try to don you my cleaning assistant.

We're all messy sometimes; and some days, it's more important to get on with the day and go play outside than it is to neatly make your bed. And, I understand that some people, especially creative artsy types (including Dad), thrive in clutter and some amount of disarray. If a little magic cleaning elf snuck in one night to stack, sort, and toss, clearing some space, they'd likely fill it all up again the next day. So you might be a messy type or a neat freak, and I'll strive to accept and understand you if it's the former…but I hope you'll learn to take care of and pride in your physical space.

~Mom

When someone says something mean to you

At some point in your life, someone will say
something mean to you. Like I explained when I
wrote to you about my childhood, as relatively easy
as I had it, it's pretty much a given that growing up
includes some amount of trauma and damage, even
when it's nobody's fault or intent. Pain is
inevitable—physical and emotional—and that's not
all bad or scary. Without it, life would be boring and
we wouldn't really appreciate happiness and pleasure;
nor would we have much reason or opportunity to
grow in spirit and strength.

Some people work to heal their pain and
minimize ways in which their own wounds inflict
new wounds on the people they touch. Some don't
cope or heal as well, and instead they take their pain
out on others. If someone ever tells you that you are
ugly or stupid, or picks on something unique about
you, it's likely because they are unaware...of their
own heart, and of yours. It's not an excuse or free
pass for their behavior, but it's important to
understand their meanness comes from an unconscious place. They aren't actually thinking about
you. They just don't feel good, about themselves,
their lives, or the damage that's been inflicted upon
them. And they get some fleeting respite from all

that sadness—maybe even a misguided sense of power—when they point their finger outward.

But when you're young, and even when you're older and fully understand this on a logical level, it still hurts. When someone says something mean to you, I hope you will come to me. I'll hold you, and you can cry about it for as long as you need to. Then I'll remind you that the someone was speaking from a place of hurt. And I will try to nurture in you a balance between forgiveness and standing up for yourself, between compassion and confidence. While I'm sure all of this sounds lovely, just know that part of me will be thinking, "People suck." And your dad will be plotting ways to...uh... "instill some consciousness in them," if you will.

The reality is you will know bullies, even if you aren't their target. You will meet mean people. Not everyone will like you. Even people who like you will hurt you at some point. Try to let their energy roll over you rather than enter into you. Try to appreciate how complex everyone is, how much we don't understand about the personal pains and inner worlds of one another. Try to remember that some people may not love themselves enough to be very good at loving others. Most important, love yourself, flaws and all, and be kind, and be aware.

~Mom

About my first memory...

It seems like I should remember my life before
learning to tie my shoes, but no matter how quietly I
sit and think or how many family photo albums I flip
through, I draw a total blank (except for that first
dream I told you about) until one afternoon when I
was five. We were at our lake house in Walden,
Texas. Your grandparents sold the place while I was
still young, so it only exists for me the way I knew it
then: a fairytale two-story dark brown wooden
house, with rooms covered in deep blue carpet, a loft
where Parker and I would make pillow forts, and a
huge beige sectional sofa in the living room. Floor to
ceiling windows looked out over the rolling green
lawn that was always neatly mowed and soft on our
bare feet. Past the yard was our boat dock and Lake
Conroe. Chip's always loved to tell the story of the
time a contractor came over to do some work and
remarked, "Hell, that ain't no boat dock...that's a
party deck!" It was big.

One sunny summer day, family friends were over,
and the older kids and I, their little mascot of sorts,
were out on the "party deck" fishing for perch. I
hated catching the fish, watching them squirm in
pain and holding their slimy bodies down with our
feet while we removed the bloody hooks from their
mouths. But I loved fishing: the smell of lake water

on the breeze, Chip's homemade mix tapes playing on the boom box, snacks of Fritos and Coke. I had to go to the bathroom, so I scurried across the sprawling lawn into the house, not wanting to miss any of the fun while the big kids were over. When I came out of the bathroom, I noticed one of my red Keds was untied. I called Sandy over from the kitchen where she seemed to always be running the blender (margaritas, I later learned) or preparing bologna sandwiches. But she was taking too long, and I was missing all the action outside. So I sat down and tackled the intricate knot I'd been shown so many times. This time my little hands did it! I ran over to Sandy beaming with pride, and she trotted with me back out to the dock to show off to Chip, Parker and our friends.

I don't remember if they cared or celebrated with me. I just remember being happy. Apparently, this is the day I really started living, according to my memory. And what a better place to start than the lake shore under blue skies dotted with white fluffy clouds, with Placido Domingo and John Denver singing "Perhaps love is like a resting place…" on the stereo, and my brother releasing the bucket of perch back into the lake in a rare act of kindness.

Love,
Mom

When you ask how babies are made...

This is inevitable, and so it seems a question every parent should be prepared for. Some parents dread the day their innocent child asks where babies come from, as if it will be embarrassing and difficult to explain. Some begin with stories of storks or talk of God sending little baby souls from heaven down to us. I think I'm just going to give it to you straight. I don't see how it can hurt you to hear about sex, especially as your brain will likely only perceive it all at the level it's able to at any given age; your understanding of the words I say will grow appropriately as you grow.

I also, though, don't want to be one of those moms with no boundaries at all, talking to you or in front of you as if you're an adult. I've seen how that can affect children as they reach adolescence and beyond, often leading to a lack of understanding of what their own healthy boundaries should be. Most important, I don't want you to ever feel embarrassed around us. You can ask anything. I promise not to giggle awkwardly, or to make you feel like you're just a silly kid.

Even though nobody intended to hurt me, I remember well the humiliation I felt around my parents and other adults when I made (rather profound, at times) declarations or asked questions that were laughed at. One of those times was at a party my parents were hosting in our backyard one afternoon when I was rather small. I needed to ask Sandy a question. I don't recall what, and in this case I'm pretty sure it wasn't awfully meaningful, but I wanted her attention. She wasn't giving it to me because she was chatting with friends. So I poked her firmly on her breast a few times, as one might tap someone on the shoulder. I didn't know the difference between a shoulder and a boob; I just needed my mom. But laughter erupted from the guests, and Sandy's face grew red with embarrassment and even a little anger. I wanted to shrink away into oblivion.

I trust it's rare for adults to have harmful intentions when they laugh at the things kids say and do, but unless a kid is actually trying to be funny, it can feel really awful when they do. I will do my best never to inflict this confusing mortification on you.

~Mom

Dear Little Angel,

Not being able to share the enchantment of the holiday season with you is one of my greatest sorrows. Dad and I both grew up with families who loved Christmas and made it a special time for us. So we try to carry that specialness into our Christmases now. We feel like it's a time for extra beauty, reflection, ritual and celebration. It would be so lovely to experience it all with you.

On Thanksgiving night, we lug out the huge boxes of decorations from the shed. We start with the outdoor lights. I learned about exterior Christmas lighting from my dad, but I have to say...I've far surpassed Chip's expertise. Admittedly, putting up the outdoor lights isn't always *fun*. It's not unusual for family arguments to break out in dealing with all the strings that don't work each year, the tangles of lights, confusion over which extension cord goes where, and the occasional artistic difference of opinion. But Dad and I have gotten better about sorting it out over the years—he usually lights up his dry-stacked rock walls with great meticulousness and pride, and I handle the shrubs and trees. If you were with us, you could help with either, or go back and forth between us. Or you could just sit on the porch drinking hot chocolate—even though it's often about eighty degrees in the hill country in November—watching as we cover the yard in twinkles.

The next day I go to work on the inside of the house. Dad doesn't get as involved with this part, lest he make a mistake in the placement of a reindeer messing up my master design plan…but we love to blast our favorite Christmas albums we've been waiting all year to hear, taking turns choosing which is next. It's a time when togetherness matters even more than usual, even if I'm the one whisking through the house like a tornado of Christmas spirit while he sits in the middle of it sipping his margarita. So, within twenty-four hours, we've created the winter wonderland we'll enjoy for the next month.

We wait a week or so to get the tree because they only stay soft and green for so long. Choosing the perfect tree was a huge family undertaking growing up, as we'd wander the lot for hours comparing and contrasting, but Nathan has helped me learn to pick one more quickly, knowing we will love it no matter what. (It's not the only time he reminds me of Charlie Brown.) I always put the lights on because Sandy was an expert at that and taught me. How I wish I could pass along this talent to you. I would show you how to bury the strings deep in the branches, to place the lights randomly so that you can't tell there are actual strands or wires. The effect is that the lights glow from within the tree; they are part of it. Next, we put the ornaments on together, recalling stories of where each one came from.

Then it's time for celebrations with friends and family, time to reach out to people we might not have talked to in a while, time to work through our library of Christmas movies. Nearly every day involves some kind of festivity…and the invention of new holiday cocktails with pepperminty and nutmeggy flavors. I also enjoy some quiet moments alone during this season. I liked that even as a child. When Chip, Sandy, and Parker would all leave for an errand, I used to dash to the record player and put on John Denver and the Muppets' *A Christmas Together,* cranking the volume and singing along with Kermit about the Christmas star he's never seen but believes in because he feels the light burning inside. I realize it's a Muppet singing, but that song remains my favorite, and I still crank the volume and sing along to this day when I'm alone—except it's a CD now, not a record. Often tears will come to my eyes as I think about past Christmases, and all the joys and sorrows that have come and gone over the years.

For Dad, the holidays can be an especially sad time, because he can't help but think of how much he misses Sierra if she's not with us…and all those years he couldn't be with her on Thanksgiving or Christmas Day. It's just one more reason we would so love to celebrate with you, together as a family, like Dad always wished he could with your sister. The holiday season can make us wistful, remind us of losses, sometimes even make us feel lonely; it has a way of tuning us in more deeply than usual to all of our feelings. Understand though, I'm not talking about everyone. For a lot of people Christmas is not a big deal, or they've dismissed it as overly commercial. Many would scoff at all this sentimental nonsense. But nobody in our family would, and that's all that matters.

So, I've told you about our Christmastime. What I will never know is the delight of making it special for you. Just as so many other feelings are amplified during this time of year, I am more aware of missing you then, because as much as I still love it all, I long for the chance to witness the yuletide merriment and wonder only a child can really feel.

Growing up, Parker and I did a special craft every day of December. We made chains of red and green construction paper rings, so we could tear one off every day we got closer to the 25th. We wrote our letters to Santa. Then on Christmas Eve, we would drive to Navasota, about an hour away from Houston, to celebrate with Chip's side of the family. Later, on the drive back, I would look at the starry sky wondering where Santa's sleigh might be. Once we were home, after getting into pajamas, Parker and I would each get to open one present before Chip and

Sandy sent us to bed. I always slept in Parker's room that night. Not that we actually slept. We were just too excited. And I swear, sometimes we heard reindeer bells on the roof. We always woke up to find signs that Santa had been there. The cookies and milk were gone, the reindeer food we'd left out had been nibbled on, and there was an array of new gifts under our ten-foot tall Douglas fir. It may seem like a lot of the fun was about Santa and gifts, but honestly it was really about the spirit...the feeling that miracles could actually be possible. And it was about our family—how we loved to be together, and seemed to love each other just a little more during this time. It was about forming traditions. The thought that these will die out with me is almost unbearable. So, maybe I'll put that Muppets Christmas CD in, listen to Kermit sweetly singing, and instead think of that star "shining from afar" whether we can see it or not. And maybe you can understand why this might offer me some comfort.

Merry Christmas darling,
Mom

If man is not to stifle his human feelings, he must practice kindness towards animals, for he who is cruel to animals becomes hard also in his dealings with men. We can judge the heart of a man by his treatment of animals.

~ Immanuel Kant

If you ever hurt an animal...

There are countless unknowns about any person coming into this world: intellect, sexuality, physical makeup, interests, strengths and weaknesses. Some of the unknowns are scary, but I imagine the parental instinct would make it quite easy to love and support you no matter how you turn out. But...my parental instinct would be drastically challenged if my child exhibited a disregard for life of any form, especially those who have no defense or way to speak up to us humans.

My logical self knows most children are likely to hurt or kill some kind of critter before they understand or know better, but if my offspring were to do so purposely, flippantly, or worse...just for the sake of killing, I will be distraught. Some humans feel superior to other species. They feel like our ability to talk and use tools (or something?) makes us better, giving us the right to treat those others as if their existence matters less. We often use and abuse them rather than consider them as the sentient beings they are. This is one view, or way of thinking and acting, that I can be bold enough to simply say is wrong... and I do not use that word, or make any judgment, lightly.

I know you may not have the same passion for animal advocacy and welfare as I. You may not want to ride horses. You may not beg for your own dog or cat. Or heaven forbid, you may have allergies to animals. That would make me sad, but I can deal. However, I *can't* abide in my child disrespect for another life, no matter how small or inconsequential it may seem.

So, if you hurt another creature, I will ask you to consider why any of our lives should be more significant than any other. I'll ask you to try to put yourself in the shoes...or paws, or hooves, or antennae...of the animal you have harmed. I'll ask you to talk about how it feels when you hurt or kill something. I might be expecting too much. I might be asking you to understand more than you can or ought to. I never said I would be a good mom, or even a mediocre one. But as your mom, I will ask this of you: Give every life thought and consideration. Treat the smallest and weakest on this planet how you would want to be treated. When any being comes across your path or into your care, treasure that responsibility and all the opportunities it gives you to make the world a more compassionate and peaceful place.

Thank you sweet girl,
Mom

by Norma Brown

My daughter,

Something I should explain is why these letters are addressed to my daughter, not "my child" or "my son." One reason for my choice not to have you is the risk that you may in fact be a boy. It's not that I have anything against men. I actually prefer their company, albeit the older ones, the ones who have outgrown some of their boyishness. Ironically, as I've told you, I was a total tomboy as a kid. I didn't mind a game of four-square with my girlfriends during recess, but I often preferred to arm-wrestle or play football. I liked doing the guy stuff, but that didn't mean boys were easy to be around.

Parker was my most constant playmate in the early years, largely out of necessity (he was my brother…he was there). And we did have fun— inventing our own summer and winter Olympics competitions each year, exploring the bayou nearby, romping all over the neighborhood together. Still, he drove me crazy. He could be mean. He wasn't very sensitive. He couldn't be happy playing alone, which meant I was always on call. He loved to make fun of me and rile me up. I officially decided I "hated" him when I was about eight or nine. Don't worry, as we grew up, we slowly became close again, and I love my big brother dearly today. It seems my experience with him was just part of my love-hate relationship with boys. And of course I'm grateful I grew up with a brother, as I can't imagine who I'd be otherwise. But let me be careless with my stereotyping for a moment. Boys are louder, often less thoughtful and empathetic (at least on the outside), dirtier, rougher, and sometimes more violent and angry. They are little storms of energy. They like to destroy and conquer. I can't relate to these things. A little boy's inclination to behave with reckless abandon, however valid and natural it might be, isn't something I know how to nurture and guide.

Of course there are boys like your dad was. He was always peaceful and thoughtful. He didn't feel at home in "recklessness," and he would rather strum his guitar or wander the woods alone than play video games or shoot birds with BB guns. Obviously, I know boys can be delightful and adorable. And, as I said, especially once they hit a certain age when their bodies and brains have settled a little (like forty-ish?), I find male energy to often be more fun and simple to be around. I just feel especially unqualified to raise a boy. And since the task of parenting seems daunting enough, and since I can choose in my fantasy world, I choose you...my daughter.

Love,
Mom

On your twelfth birthday,

This is my last "happy birthday" to a little girl.
You're about to be a teenager. Terrifying. Sandy tells
me that at some point in my twelfth year, when I was
in sixth grade, a switch flipped in me and I went to
bed one night a happy-go-lucky sweet kid and woke
up a grumpy, stoic teenager. And that was it, for
about ten years. She's not wrong. I did get moody,
and you're likely to as well. It's those darn hormones.
And I think it's also that our worlds get a lot bigger
as we get older, and it can be overwhelming. We
used to be content in our little bubble of family, toys,
home, and a few good friends. Our needs were fairly
simple. But then you have to start worrying about
grades, and boys, and bodies, and dances, and who
likes you and who doesn't, and beliefs and values,
and desires (some confusing, some exciting, some
torturous). Not only all that, but you're tired all the
time. School, homework, sports, teams, and hobbies
don't allow for the sleep a growing girl needs. Twelve
was the age my bed became my sanctuary and I
became a world-class napper.

I shouldn't be a rain cloud on your special day,
though, so let me brighten this up a bit. I have loved
each and every birthday I've had, so excited to get
older and learn more and know more and see what
new opportunities, wisdom, and experiences await

me. I hope you start off your twelfth year with great excitement. I hope your creative outlets, moments of solitude, and experiences in nature continue to provide you with peace as you navigate the oh so complicated territory of adolescence. I hope we have helped you cultivate a strong self-love that will remain with you no matter who else out there loves you or doesn't. And I hope you will not feel too grown-up now to snuggle, and to seek solace and comfort from Mom and Dad whenever the world feels like too much.

Happy happy day!!

~Mom

*Sometimes, if you stand on the bottom rail of a bridge and
lean over to watch the river slipping slowly away beneath you,
you will suddenly know everything there is to be known.*

~ A.A Milne

To my flower-child,

We would want to raise you "where the wild things
are." I don't mean the storybook jungle full of big
beasts to conquer. I mean we'd want you surrounded
by the birds, butterflies, cats, deer, crawly critters,
flowers, rivers, and skies that make up our outdoor
home here in the hill country of Texas. I would want
you to be just as comfortable lying on the ground
under a blanket of stars as in your cozy bed under a
soft cotton blanket. I would want you to take
comfort from trees swaying in the wind. I would
want you to feel peace and inspiration in the silence
of nature. There is actually so much to hear in the
silence—the absence of man-made noise—that many
wise people consider an endangered "species." I
would want you to get dirty and sweaty, to play
games with bugs and talk to the plants…and yes,
maybe even to hug trees.

   I would want you to explore. When you're young,
this is probably not going to be hard to encourage.
It's in our nature…to be in nature. Little ones seem

to always want to be out in it—in the rain and puddles, the snow, the sun and sand. And because I know I should do it more often myself, I'd even let you play outside barefoot, with no barrier between you and the earth (we'll just have to wipe our feet off before we go inside). We'd strap you to our backs on hikes when you're a baby, and as you get older... even in your teens...I hope you would want to continue to join us out there. And I hope you would go out on your own, unearthing new wild things all around you and inside yourself. Why do I believe this is so important? Just listen, and the river will tell you...

Love,
Mom

To my favorite Facebook friend,

There is no overstating how detrimental I believe social media and iPhones, our constant "plugged-in-ed-ness," can be for children, and adults actually. The World Wide Web, i.e. the Internet, didn't exist to the public until 1991. I was sixteen when I sent my first email and thirty when I got my first "smart" phone. I am grateful for that. I cannot imagine raising a child who has access to anything and everything via Google—all that you'll be able to see and "learn" without my knowledge or supervision...perhaps before your impressionable little brain is able to process what you are seeing. The mind boggles at the billions of images and bits of information all there within reach of a few clicks.

And then there's the overwhelming pressure of keeping up with what everyone's doing and saying online. How can I arm you against the insidious "FOMO" (fear of missing out) fostered by the constant sharing at the fingertips of every kid with a phone or Facebook profile? I will try my damnedest to keep an iPhone out of your hands for as long as possible. I daresay that even means refusing to succumb to the temptation to hand you ours to entertain you when we're dining out in restaurants or doing other boring adult things. I will insist that we take text-free, Instagram-less vacations. I will make you keep your computer in the living room so you don't get any private time with it. I don't know when I'll have to give in, when it will become cruel and unusual punishment to keep you unplugged and disconnected. I don't know if my refusal to get with the times will cause you other sorts of problems and have its own set of consequences.

On a positive note, just like in so many other ways, I can see how the responsibility of being your mom will force me to be better. It will force me to model moderation of all the screen-time and connectivity, to care less what news I'm missing on Facebook and more about what you're doing right in front of me. I promise you won't find Dad and me staring at our phones during mealtimes, instead of talking or just being comfortable in shared silence. We're already relatively careful about this, recognizing the powerful draw of the blue screen's easy access to email and texts and updates about whomever we're not with at the moment. But sometimes Dad will immediately get out his phone when we get in my car to go somewhere, and I instantly feel the disconnect—he's doing something else while sitting right beside me, rather than having to make conversation or just being there with me in the passenger seat. And sometimes the chime of a few text messages arriving on my phone while we're enjoying a quiet night at home makes him wonder whom else I'd rather be talking to than him, right there together in our living room. So we could use a reminder to be better. With you we will strive to be present in every moment, rather than preoccupied with posting and sharing those moments with our friends and "friends." I hope.

We humans have had little time to adjust to the ubiquity of wi-fi. We're fumbling our way through, unsure of the benefits, dangers, and consequences. And I'll have no idea, I'm afraid, how to guide you in this new reality. This new iWorld.

~Mom

When you tell me you hate me...

I'm quite certain that you will tell me this one day. It may not be until those temperamental teenage years, but it will happen, if you're anything like I was: impatient, passionate, stubborn. It may happen when I tell you I have doubts about one of your friends, or I demand that you get off the phone late at night, or I don't let you do what all the other kids are doing. Sandy heard it from me for a range of "offenses" from insisting on keeping a part-time job when it was clear to me it only made her stressed and grumpy, to expressing concern that I was depressed when I was sixteen (I actually thought myself rather happy...just put out by annoying family members). Obviously, I didn't hate my mom, and you won't hate me. I was just angry at what I felt was unfair. While I hope to teach you more constructive ways to deal with anger, it is not a bad thing when we allow it to be and then move on from it. It can reveal what matters to us. So, I think I can take it, when you tell me you hate me. I might even reply with an ever-so-annoying, "Well, I *love* you."

~Your exasperating mother

Laughing as much as possible, playing in nature, meditating, writing, and nurturing my relationships keeps me in alignment. We all bloom into our intended states given the right nutrients and tender care. Gratitude, connection, self-love, and living with purpose keep us growing towards our guiding light.

~ Sarah Hernandez

About a friend like Sarah...

I wish for you a friend like my Sarah. I met her in kindergarten and we became best friends within days. I can't recall why, but I imagine it had a lot to do with two things that remain true today: we make each other laugh like crazy, and we are absolutely comfortable with one another in a way that is so rare. Even back then, we were nothing alike. I was a fairly reserved boyish girl with an older brother. She was a bold, bouncy, beautiful girlish girl with two older sisters. She was quite popular from the start, and that remained true through our thirteen years at the private prep school that I've told you I loved even though the homogeny and snobbery posed some challenges. Sarah was silly and charming, and boys (and girls alike) were drawn to her aura. I envied her, as I had plenty of friends but lacked her awesome inherent magnetism.

When we were in sixth grade, and the hormones kicked in along with the popularity contest and pressures of middle school, I decided I finally wanted to learn how to be like a girl, and she gave me a makeover, teaching me how to put my hair back in a bow and wear jewelry. But she never made me feel like anything was wrong with how I'd been up until then. I loved school and sports and was disciplined about both; Sarah...not so much. We were on all the same t-ball and softball teams, but while I really wanted to win, she just wanted to have fun. We did run cross-country together from sixth grade through twelfth, and neither of us took that very seriously. We just spent the whole time trying not to throw up or fall down. I was careful and methodical about most things; she was a bit reckless, in an endearing way. (Sandy will tell you to this day that if Sarah was coming over, we all knew to expect some spillage or minor property damage.)

In high school, Sarah was part of the cool crowd and she partied with them. While I was friendly enough with that group, I didn't "mix" with them on the weekends as I was a teetotaler and all around "good girl." Sarah had a string of constant boy-friends starting in fifth grade. I had my first when I went away for a brief exchange program at sixteen, and my second the next year. In other words, my romantic life was a lot more limited, and of course, I also envied her that.

So, what did we have in common? We were both genuinely nice people (except for the occasional slip-up in middle school when "mean girl" mentality can overcome the most benevolent of us). We loved our friends and families and pets. We loved to make up new games. We loved to talk. And oh how we laughed. At anything. At nothing. Uncontrollable, gut-shaking, breath-taking laughter. We laughed at TV shows, we laughed on stage during choir performances, we laughed in church (for a year or two, we decided to go to church together on Sunday evenings, just the two of us). And if there wasn't something to laugh about, we invented it. We gave each other silly names like "Coffee" and "Cream." We moved our stuffed animals around in enter-taining dances and gave them funny faces. We passed each other notes with gossip written in bits of French ("Elle est pénible!") we figured nobody else could understand since we were the only among our friends who chose to take French instead of Spanish.

Most important—and why I wish for you a Sarah—as we grew up together, and life started to get more serious, we were able to talk about anything without embarrassment and we could always feel safe in each other's love and acceptance of the people we were and things we did. We have always really *seen* each other, and this is a treasure in a relationship—we're all searching for this deep satisfaction of being seen and often don't find it.

Sarah started to have a tough time around thirteen. I didn't know it yet, but her father was very unstable (undiagnosed and untreated bipolar disorder, we would later understand), and he could go from being her best friend and the coolest dad around to abusing his family and yelling horrible criticisms at Sarah. As his toxicity came more and more to the forefront, Sarah also began to struggle with what would take years to be diagnosed as bipolar. While I didn't understand the extent of her pain, she was able to talk to me through it all...and when she was ready to tell a friend that she had been cutting and hurting herself, she told me. I witnessed her cope with years of depression, a very long process of having to eliminate her father from her life, going to college and dropping out over and over, and even her attempts to end her own life.

I've watched her go through all this, seeing that no matter how she struggled she was always a kind, loving, empathetic, and loyal friend, daughter, and sister. She was so caring in fact, her respect for the feelings of her family and friends is often what prevented her from harming herself. I watched her ultimately get a graduate degree and become an amazingly strong, talented woman and successful therapist. She is happy and married, and she wants to be a mom so badly. I'm grateful that this means I may get the chance to be an aunt. She has also been there for me throughout any and all drama, divorce, self-doubts, and life's celebrations and sorrows. There are many things I have thought or experienced that I will tell only Sarah. And often, things don't seem real until I do share them with her and hash them out. She is my sounding board, my grounding force, my advisor, my confidante.

So...it's not about what we've done for each other. It's what we've been able to be for each other. I wish for you a friend you can have your whole life, someone who is your safe place, someone who will want the best for you every day of your life.

Much love,
Mom

About a friend like Elizabeth...

I wish for you a friend like Elizabeth. She wasn't a
"lifer" at our school, so our friendship doesn't go
back quite as far, but as soon as she moved from the
East Coast to Houston and joined us in fifth grade,
we became fast friends. It was likely our silliness and
ability to laugh together that first sparked our friendship—just like with Sarah, but as our interests and
natures were similar in many ways, our relationship
quickly deepened and continued throughout middle
and high school. We were alike in that we always
wanted to do our best in school, in sports, and in any
endeavor. She was (and is) terribly smart, and lots of
stuff in school came to her more naturally than it did
to me; this pushed me to study harder. I wanted to
do as well as she did, be as good as she was. I remember one time in sixth grade when we stayed up
until 3 a.m. working on a Nixon/Reagan debate
project for History class, totally delirious by the end
of the night. We simply didn't know how to half-ass
something when we were doing it together. And we
made it fun.

When we were in ninth grade, together we con-
vinced our school to start its first girls' lacrosse team.
But we both loved track, so again together we
persuaded the athletic department to allow us to
participate in two simultaneous varsity sports,

something that was unheard of. That only lasted for one year before Elizabeth chose track, and I chose lacrosse…one of the more difficult moments in our friendship (and I'm not kidding). Like me, she chose to be vice-free in high school, so we grew even closer then as we would spend weekends memorizing movie lines (our favorites were anything Tom Cruise was in) or chatting through the night while others were out partying in another way.

She became an investment banker in New York and had three children. So, I don't get to see her as much as I'd like in our adult years. But we pick up wherever we left off when we do unite—there is no awkwardness or phoniness. I know I could count on her if I ever needed anything. And it's been fascinating watching her as a mother. She loves motherhood but acknowledges the difficulties, as she's a genuine and down-to-earth person. She recently told me she thinks it's courageous to choose not to have children, because it means having to put more thought into what my life is all about, into my purpose—because once you have kids, they are your given purpose. That was such an insightful way to articulate much of what I'd been considering over the years…whether I might have things I want to do *more* than parent, and if so, what are they? While Elizabeth's children are her life's primary purpose and priority, I've been amazed by how hard she's continued to work (because she loves it) and balance it all. She's actually one of my only close friends who does have children, and seeing someone I've known and loved since she was eleven be a parent can make me wistful. But when Dad and I stayed in their living room in Tribeca, and her two-year old twins would scream for hours at bedtime, waking at 6 a.m. to stare at us on the pullout sofa asking, "Mama, why are they sleeping?," I was less wistful.

I have always admired and respected Elizabeth. We remain similar in many ways—in our stoic and practical nature; our devotion to family and friends; our ability to find humor in any situation. It's just that now she's a banker in New York and mother of three, and I'm an professor in Texas and mother of two cats and a dog.

I wish for you a friend like her because we were so alike, because we inspired each other to work harder and do better, and because having her in my corner has always made me feel safer and reassured. We have a shared history that will always connect us. It's these friends you make early on and stick with forever, for good reason, that can make a big difference in your life and outlook. They provide stability just like family, but in ways that are unique from what parents can provide. I have made many different types of friends in my adult life, a few who have become family to me and have sustained me in similar ways as these old friends. I could write pages and pages on each of them. I don't need to wish them for you, though, because if you have this foundation that comes from maintaining old friendships, I'm quite sure you'll find the new.

Love,
Mom

About following the rules...

As I've already touched on, I was a pretty darn good kid growing up. I typically wanted to do the "right thing," and not because I was given a lot of rules and restrictions by my parents. In fact, I think bed times were the only overtly stated rules. Perhaps this was just Sandy and Chip's parenting style...perhaps it was because we were generally well-behaved and thus didn't need many rules...perhaps they trusted us and had a laid back attitude about us making our own mistakes...or maybe it was a combination of all of the above. Regardless, I didn't need rules to motivate me to be and do good.

In college I began to drink and have never looked back, and I even experimented very occasionally with certain drugs. My guideline was that I was open to it "as long as it grew from the ground," so that allowed for things like mushrooms and pot. Technically, the underage drinking and drug use meant I broke the law. Relatively speaking, though, I've been an upright citizen. Still, I become overly nervous when cops are around lest they find something amiss in my behavior (as a kid, I always tensed up when a policeman was eating at a restaurant where we were, thinking they could arrest me if I created any disruption or committed some kind of dining-out crime). Previous to my college-life offenses, the only crimes I com-

mitted that I recall transpired solely due to the
influence and pressure of your uncle Parker, or
Sarah. I think the most heinous occurred on a quiet
summer day in my neighborhood.

Sarah was over and we were looking for something to do. We went for what I thought would be a
wholesome bike ride around the block. Sarah (I'm
totally sure she was the mastermind) decided we
should collect (one might say steal?) the mail out of
the mailboxes of my neighbors. I hesitated, but we
proceeded to ride from mailbox to mailbox quickly
swiping the contents of each. We pedaled home
excitedly, closed the door to my room, and began
tearing through all that mysterious adult mail. It
turned out to be mostly boring bills. Not very
thrilling, in the end. After Sarah was gone, there was
a knock on the front door. Sandy answered and
called to me to confront our neighbor, a nice lady I
knew, while she explained she'd seen me through her
kitchen window and told me what a serious thing I'd
done. What embarrassment and shame I felt, standing before the prosecuting party fully guilty, with
nothing to say but "I'm sorry." I can try to redeem
myself by explaining I had no idea taking mail from
another's box is a federal offense. I knew not what I
did! Still, it was pretty stupid.

I believe the "crimes" I committed with Parker
were to do with a similar ignorance and disregard for

our surroundings. Maybe a ball we (he) threw broke a neighbor's car window; maybe we would trespass in somebody's backyard as we made our way to the bayou to play. But I (I'll not speak for him) was never out to do anything wrong, and it wasn't for fear of punishment because I honestly don't remember ever being punished—scolded here and there, but not punished. I just didn't enjoy the feeling of being bad.

Because this was my nature, and I did just fine without curfews or lectures about right and wrong from my parents, what would I do if I had a rebel child? What if you *do* get your thrills out of breaking the rules? How would I tame you? How would I keep you in line? I would be totally lost, having no compass with which to understand a child or teenager who feels a pull toward danger. Even when I occasionally try to impose my ever-so-reasonable thinking in conversations your dad and I have about Sierra when she's tangled up in a mess, he has to remind me most kids aren't like I was, and that my insights aren't especially helpful to someone with a different disposition. Of course he doesn't know what to do about it all either or how to handle witnessing his child make mistakes; mostly he just realizes there's not much to *do* except love her and hope for the best. We can know this logically, but I still see how he hurts and worries for her.

Some parents seem so patient and cool, calm and collected even through their child's run-ins with the law, failures in school, and reckless transgressions. I admire them, and when I was a teacher, I could offer my fair share of support to the kids making questionable choices because their fate wasn't in my hands; they weren't my responsibility. As a parent, though, I honestly just don't think I'd be much good in dealing with the bad.

~Good Mom

by Nathan Brown

My growing girl,

Let's continue this discussion about the dangerous
stuff. I wonder if I'll already have an idea of what to
expect from you when you reach the age—which is
drastically different from one kid to the next—when
you realize you have decisions to make about drugs,
alcohol, cigarettes, and sex. Is it the years leading up
to adolescence that dictate how we'll approach these
decisions, or do we handle each temptation, opportunity, and danger as they present themselves? As I
said, my choices about these were not big hard
righteous ones; for the most part they weren't
dictated by authority or religion. They either came
from within or by example. Chip smoked cigarettes,
and Parker and I both grew up hating the smell.
Thankfully, Sandy forced him to do all his smoking
outside. We always wanted him to quit, and there
was no way I was ever going to put a cigarette in my
mouth. Chip and Sandy rarely drank at home; alcohol
wasn't around and was never a temptation, even in
high school.

What I appreciate about that, besides the fact that
it likely kept me out of a plethora of precarious pos-
itions, is that I always knew how to make my own
fun with my friends, or alone. I didn't want or need
the warm buzz of alcohol to ease my inhibitions or
make a Friday night more exciting. I was perfectly

entertainable without it. Now that I do like adult beverages, I actually miss the days when I was blissfully ignorant to the pleasures of wine, cosmos, margaritas... (Martinis are my favorite, but I like it all. Family and friends marvel at my ability to drink like a fish—a skinny, healthy one—with no effects other than a slightly more chatty demeanor.) While I enjoy the buzziness, I also admit that I lean on alcohol as a crutch to assuage boredom, to loosen up, to lubricate conversation. I'd like for you to go as long as possible without that crutch.

Sex was a little more complicated. Even when I was very young, I always had a longing for this mysterious, seemingly delicious part of being grown-up. Again, I can't recall a single conversation about the act or ethics and safety surrounding it at home. Our eighth grade "Decisions for Healthy Living" class taught us the basics of the biology and STDs, but that was it. In high school, I did have my stint with Young Life and Christianity that made it quite clear that you wait until marriage to have sex, and I bought into that for the most part. All along, though, since I did feel temptation and curiosity, perhaps what really "saved" me was the lack of opportunity. When, in my senior year of high school, I finally had a boyfriend, he was devoted to his Jewish faith that also called on horny teens to wait. So that was that. By the time I got to college, I had left Young Life and religion behind, and after months of careful consideration, I took the plunge with the guy I then loved. I never left behind, however, my belief that sex is a serious and complicated act best reserved for people who have serious and complicated feelings for one another. At the very least, it's damn intimate…and when you share that level of intimacy with someone, you'd better be ready for all that comes with it.

If I have a point in this letter, I think it's this: I was largely shielded from danger and damage from these "vices," for lack of a better word, through my disposition and environment. I don't know how to shield you because I can't control your disposition or even really your environment as much as I wish I could. I'm guessing there are some things I can't protect you from, ways in which I have to let go and let you "use your own poor judgment" as Grandpa always says…though that is drastically easier to say than to do. So let me just share this little piece of motherly wisdom (I know, I know): all of these choices are about *your* body and *your* mind. Your body and mind take a long time to develop. So, I hope you respect both enough to nurture their development by keeping the early destructive forces on them to a minimum. That is all.

~Scared Mom

About the funny stuff...

The telling...and retelling...and retelling...of funny family stories never gets old when we gather together. The stories and the laughter connect us. Parker and I might be as different as night and day, but we've always giggled together whenever we recall Chip's reaction of disgust all those time we snuck buttermilk into his glass at dinner, Sandy's insistence on shamelessly belting out songs in her distinct operatic style throughout the house when we were growing up, or the infamous night Parker snuck in my room with a tape recorder to capture me snoring after my insistence I never snored (he laughs more about that).

I wish you could have known your great-grandfather Bill, Chip's dad. He was fun-loving, kind, and good with kids. When I was little, I forgave his gross cigarette and cigar smoking, and I didn't notice the temper he occasionally had with my grandmother Maxine when he'd had a few whiskeys at night. To me, he was wonderful. He taught us to play dominoes and solitaire and made us coffee with cream and sugar at night. Much to our delight, he sang "Goodnight, ladies..." over and over when it was time for bed, never actually caring if we went to bed or not.

Max was equally loving. One way she expressed her love was through making us treats. A favorite was chocolate pudding. If our times with them sound a little unhealthy nutritionally speaking, they probably were. But what else are grandparents for? One evening, they were taking care of Parker and me along with our cousin Laura. We excitedly went to the kitchen fridge to procure our puddings and each grabbed a glass dish with an individual serving. As kids tend to get giddy when they're staying somewhere special—and have had coffee—we decided to merrily swing our pudding dishes upside down on the way to the living room; after all, pudding always had that congealed layer on top keeping everything in place. But when cousin Laura enthusiastically swung her dish, the chocolate goo splattered everywhere: the linoleum kitchen floor, the adjacent living room carpet, the walls. Her pudding was a goner. Worse yet, Bill came in to see what the ruckus was about, and upon seeing the pudding disaster yelled, "What a *goddamn* mess!" An outburst like that isn't easy to take for an impressionable little girl who just wanted her grandma's pudding. Laura ran sobbing out the back door and, as far as we knew, away forever (after much shouting and cajoling from the balcony, Max managed to get her back home). Parker guffawed the whole time. Max cleaned up the goddamn mess, I suppose. I ate my pudding.

Now, we laugh every time we think of it...
knowing, of course, that cousin Laura recovered and
went on to live a happy life. If anyone spills or breaks
something, it always eases the tension to recall Bill's
words and to repeat them with ever-increasing
histrionics: WHAT...A...**GOD...DAMN**...MESS!

~Mom

What I don't want to pass along...

I am happy to tell you that I love, and even like, myself. I may not be for everybody. I'm not saying I'm especially great. Some things about me surely annoy, or even anger, my loved ones, friends, and acquaintances. But at the end of the day, if we are true to ourselves and genuinely care about how we impact this world and those around us, I sure hope we go to bed loving ourselves, quirks and all. Having said that, there are some things about myself maybe I'd rather not pass along to you.

I'm not going to worry about the physical stuff. I'll get into body image issues in another letter, but for all my early lamenting and self-consciousness about my bird legs, an upturned nose, and freckles, I have even come to love my outward appearance. I am grateful for it. What a shame it would be to criticize my own healthy and perfectly able body because certain features may not be on trend. So...you may have all my lankiness, my hairy arms, and my knobby knees.

What I'd rather you not inherit is my indecisiveness. My meekness. My self-centeredness. My uptightness.

I could easily defend all four qualities; I've grown quite accustomed to them, and we tend to latch onto what we're used to. But indecisiveness may indicate a weak connection to intuition. It's also just plain stressful when I lack a clear idea of what I want or what I should do...like...to have children or not. I would like for you to have strong intuition and the confidence to follow it.

Meekness can lead us to do things we know aren't best for us, or even those we love, because we want to please or are too shy to speak up. A meek attitude can trick us into thinking everyone knows more or better than we do. Admittedly, there are many times and areas in life where I am not meek at all, but along the way, the tendency has held me back and caused me to make some mistakes. I want you to value your own judgments and ideas, and to act on those without apology.

Self-centeredness can cause me to think people in the grocery store line really ought to speed up because it's clear I'm in a hurry. Or it can cause me to hurt your dad because I think my preferences, pleasures, and pains are more important than his. Or it can simply trick me into thinking my little problems actually matter in the big scheme of things, when really we're all just lucky to be part of this extraordinarily large universe. While I want you to respect and value yourself, I hope you are also humble and realize nothing revolves around you.

I've been pretty uptight for as long as I can remember, and it's really done nothing but cause useless anxiety and irk friends and family. It's never been easy for me to go with the flow, even when the flow comes from the current of my favorite people. I think I am overly concerned with being comfortable (physically, socially, and emotionally) at all times. I want to know what's coming, to be in control, to know I am safe. So, I fear my uptight nature may be all about just that: fear. In fact, little one, this fear of not having control is likely the trait that prevails in my decision not to have you. I want *you* to be able to plan, prepare, and take things seriously when necessary but also to be okay with some discomfort and not always knowing what's next. In other words, I hope you're a little more laid back than your mom.

Wishing you only the best parts of me,
Mom

P.S.

I forgot to mention in the last letter, I suffer from "Resting Bitch Face." I use that term reluctantly, hoping you will understand the humor in it. I actually think it's a sexist expression, but…I do kind of have it. It's a term used to describe the phenomenon of a woman's face (sometimes men's faces too, which is why I'm more accepting of the term) that looks inherently grumpy or displeased when at rest. So, when I'm doing nothing or unengaged in conversation, or even when I am working or focused, my face might imply I'm not happy.

Your dad and I have struggled with this for years, and sometimes still do. Once that initial phase of our relationship, filled with constant excitement, transitioned into the settled phase, he had a chance to see my face at rest more, and he often wondered what was wrong. Why was I so miserable? Why did I look like a bitch? (He would never say that last one, of course.) It stressed him out and frustrated me. How many times can I explain that nothing is wrong and this is just my face? It's not pleasant or flattering to be told you look unhappy. But I knew what the issue was, because people had called it to my attention before.

In college, friends would often say, "I saw you walking across campus today, and you looked so mad. Are you okay?" I was just walking, people! Strange men have told me to smile…as I ponder which olive oil to buy at the store or wait in a line. The idea that I should exert the energy to turn up the corners of my mouth, or whatever one is supposed to do to remove the "bitch" from her face, while engaging in an everyday task by myself seems absurd to me. So, on one hand, I'm fine with my face just like it is. But maybe your life will be easier if you don't inherit my RBF, so I guess I'll add that to the list.

~Mom

On being a woman...

It's ironic how I envied boyhood as a young girl because I so love being a woman and now understand I actually loved being a girl then too. So why did I want to act and play like a boy, and even look like a boy? Perhaps it's because I wanted to be strong, tough, and capable, and to use my body in physical ways; and I associated these things with boyness. On the playground, on the baseball field, or in the yard playing football with Chip and Parker I was always out to prove (even if only to myself) I could be just as fast, just as talented, just as good as the boys. Short hair and comfortable clothes made more sense to me than flowing locks and frilly dresses. Deep down, did I somehow understand that males often get more respect in society, or have more power, more choices? Or was it just a matter of tastes or the fact that I had a big brother with an intense and influential personality? I really don't know.

What I do know is that women can be active, athletic, beautiful, tough, resilient, intelligent, nurturing, empathetic, kind, multifaceted, complex humans—just as men can. I also happen to prefer my female form. Being a woman in this world isn't always easy, but neither is being a human. Shockingly and shamefully, as I write this letter, in America we are still dealing with the fact that women often don't get the same pay for the same work as men; that some people including many in our government think they have a right to limit a woman's access to and choices about her healthcare, body, and reproduction; and that we elected a man to be our president who once proudly proclaimed that due to his fame and fortune he can kiss and grab a woman on a whim, assuming they're all his for the taking.

Our media scrutinizes the physical appearance of women, and we have to constantly be aware of and to deprogram the messages we're being sent about how our value and beauty are dependent upon our looks. We're encouraged to be "sexy," because we're treated better and "get" more when we are. Simultaneously, we're often accused of seductively inviting the male gaze or inappropriately encouraging their attention. We walk a fine line between being friendly and being a pushover, being flirty and being slutty, being tough and being bitchy, being smart and being dorky, being an animal-lover and being the "crazy cat lady." (Note that you never hear about the "crazy cat man.") And I can't even get started on aging; I could write a whole other book on our societal failure to accept, value, and celebrate women as they get older.

I tell you all of this because I want you to be aware that you will have to face these challenges. But again, every human has to face a certain set. You can ask your dad about the expectations and stereotypes that even go along with being a white male, the most privileged group historically. What is most important for you to know is that being a woman—a proud, strong woman—is wonderful. I already shared with you what I'd rather not pass along to you. Now I want to tell you what makes me happy to be the woman I am...

I am sensitive and thoughtful. I look at things and people from a variety of perspectives. I foster relationships and care for others. I am smart and have the potential to be creative. I am peaceful and strive to be peace-making. I think it's amazing that I can give birth if I so choose. I think a woman's body in general is an amazing work of art. I think it's pretty great that in any given day I can mow the lawn, build a piece of furniture, go for a jog, encourage Dad to do yoga with me, clean the house, ride a horse, cook a great meal, enjoy long talks over coffee with a friend, enjoy sex, enjoy being alone, take good care of the animals, and work hard at everything I do. I try to feel just as beautiful and confident running errands around town wearing sweats and no makeup as I do going out at night with my now-very-long hair down and maybe even wearing a dress. I am still a proud tomboy and also a proud woman. And I am married to a partner who loves and appreciates all of this that is me. This is what being a woman means to me...even if I have to remind myself it is not arrogant to list the qualities I like about myself for my daughter. We don't often go around touting our favorite things about ourselves in our personal relationships, but I think it's important that you see and understand that your mom is happy with herself, that she has inherent—and earned— value. Your potential is endless. And while society at large may want to define you and your potential based on gender, it really has nothing to do with it. Be proud, and speak up. Your unique voice and identity—however you'd like to define or refrain from defining it—matter.

~Your mother

How lucky I am to have something that makes saying goodbye so hard.

~ Annie

About your canine sister...

It makes me so sad that I will never bring you home to meet Cayenne. You will never know her love and protection, her utter joy in being alive, her soothing sighs as she stretches out next to you. On the other hand (if you can't tell yet, I always have an "other hand"), my relationship with her and the dog and cats that came before her in my life are part of the reason I'm not sure I should have, or that I need, a human child. I have a deep desire and proclivity to nurture, but animals have always stirred that up in me the most.

I told you about our family dog Misha, but Honeybun was "my" first dog. She was the dog I hoped for and asked for every birthday and Christmas until I was twelve. After years of pleading, Sandy finally caved. I spent months searching, visiting shelters and reading ads. I did not take the task of choosing my companion lightly. Honeybun was a small Sheltie, the runt of her litter with a stub tail, whose family didn't want her anymore. She became my dog until I was twenty-five. She was highly intelligent, emotionally dependent, and incredibly gentle and loyal. She was always absolutely focused on me, to the point that I sometimes felt over-whelmed wondering if I was being an attentive enough "mom" to her. She didn't need a leash because she wouldn't leave my side. I thought I'd never feel a connection like that to another dog.

I adopted Cayenne from the Houston SPCA in 2005, just a couple of months after Honeybun died. As I wandered past the kennels, her sweet eyes and huge perky dingo-like ears got me. But when my ex-husband and I brought her home, I honestly thought I'd made a mistake. This crazy cattle dog mutt had no sense of loyalty. Why should she? She was a youngster someone found on the streets of Hous-ton…who knows what she'd been through or if anyone had loved her in her first months of life. She was easily distracted. She was fast, strong, and stubborn. I dreaded our walks. No matter how I trained her (and she did quickly learn many other skills), she pulled me so hard on her leash I would often feel like falling to my knees in frustration. I cried at night wondering why I adopted another dog so soon after the loss of my delicate, perfectly behaved Honeybun.

We stuck together though. Two years after bring-ing her home, my home fell apart. My husband and I divorced, and Cayenne and I moved to an apartment together…something that felt like a huge step backward in life. Years later, she would accompany me to live with Dad in Oklahoma. By that time, she had settled down. She'd grown out of her puppy years, she'd grown to trust me, and we'd grown together. In Norman, she got a yard for the first time, and a pond nearby where I could let her off the leash to run as fast as she could. Sometimes she would get what I call "the crazies" when she just ran with wild abandon, unable to control her speed or body. Her joy is contagious. I swear she can smile, and does often. She has become the only absolute constant in my life: my running partner, my napping buddy, my road trip companion, my company when Nathan hits the road for work.

She's roughly thirteen now and has slowed down just a little. She's an intuitive, sensitive, and wise soul. If I am sad, she sticks close by. If your dad or I raise our voices, she pants nervously. And, even if they are silent tears, if your dad cries, she comes from wherever she may have been in the house to stand quietly by him and place her head under his hand. In her older age, she's not crazy about change and gets a little anxious when strangers come over (she's learned from me, apparently). But the way in which she welcomed two little kittens into her family was amazing. She stood guard in the backyard over both Stoney and Dylan as we acclimated these feral rescue

cats to their new home, and it was clear her protection and reassurance helped them as much as, if
not more than, mine. While she'll bark at intruders in
our territory and playfully chase away animals that
aren't part of our pack, she wouldn't hurt a flea (unless she inadvertently licked one off herself). She is
with me more than any other being in the world. She
has taught me to be patient, to live in the moment, to
find delight in the basic pleasures of life, to stretch
and smile first thing in the morning, to breathe and
remain calm. She makes me feel like everything really
is okay.

I have been so lucky to have her as my friend and
teacher, and I'm sorry you will not come to know
her.

Love,
Cayenne's Mom

"Cayenne and Nathan" by Ashley Brown

"Honeybun" by Ashley Brown

On your sixteenth birthday,

Sixteen is a big year, in American culture at least. You get to drive, and you're entering a phase of life when you're not a kid anymore but you don't have the responsibilities of adulthood yet. While I did not get the shiny red sports car my brother got on his sixteenth, I did get my mom's hand-me-down Ford Explorer, which was more than fine with me. Loading my little carrier of ten cassette tapes into the car that morning of my birthday and driving the two-minute route to school all alone was pure ecstasy. The car isn't the point; it's the autonomy. I admit, getting a car was awesome, but don't get any ideas. Remember, I was spoiled.

At sixteen, you've likely found and started to develop some of your passions, whether in sports or music or art, or some other endeavor that will tug and pull at you for the next formative years of your life. You also probably feel very grownup, very child-like, very stressed out, very insecure, very confident, very needy, and very independent all at once. Plus, you're surrounded by other girls maturing at their own pace—some becoming more interesting and empathic and some becoming more judgmental and self-involved—and by boys who despite their best intentions are largely preoccupied with their own set of hormonal challenges.

When I was sixteen, the seeds of the type of
woman I would become were starting to sprout. I
was just getting comfortable with some quirkiness in
style and personality. I still cared a whoooollle lot
what everyone else thought of me, but I was learning
I wanted to be a little different than the standard I'd
been surrounded by most of my life. I was also
having a blast with sports and photography and thrift
store clothes (not the norm compared with the de-
signer stylings of most of my preppy peers). I have
fond memories of celebrating my birthday with a
group of close friends at Mama's Café, a Houston
restaurant that served my favorite chocolate
milkshake.

I also celebrated with my dad. When I was six,
Chip sent me a postcard from Paris, where he was on
a business trip, and he promised he would take me
there when I turned sixteen. I kept that postcard
pinned to my bulletin board for ten years. As the
birthday approached, we reassessed and he gave me
the option to go to New York City or Paris. I chose
New York (what did I know?). It was extraordinary.
I've written to you about the distance and iciness that
plagued my relationship with Chip during those
tumultuous teenage years, but that vacation was
perfect. We stayed at The Waldorf Astoria on
Central Park. We trounced all over the city, as I took
hundreds of black and white photographs with my

Pentax K1000. We went to *Phantom of the Opera* on Broadway, something I had wanted to do since I was a little girl. We dined at Tavern on the Green. We saw all the sights, including celebrities. Chip took my picture with Matthew Broderick and Sarah Jessica Parker outside of a theater. The trip will forever remain in my heart as a beautiful birthday gift, given and accepted in the spirit of family, love, adventure, and respect for the fact that I was growing up.

As far as what I can do for you or tell you on this day, I want to encourage your uniqueness even if things about you are hard for me or your friends to understand. I want to make you feel special and beautiful and to help you celebrate however you choose. My wishes are that we've all survived the challenges of teen-hood thus far and that you're feeling like you have a firm foundation from which to take off into semi-almost-young-adultness. And good lord...please, please, please, as you take off, don't ever text and drive; or eat and drive; or laugh with a friend and drive; or drive too fast in the rain.

Happy sweet sixteen, my girl!

~Mommy

Photo by Ashley Brown

So if I'm out there, or here at home
Or some days just passing through
I am here, and I am there for you

~ Nathan Brown

Dear daughter of Nathan and Ashley,

I want to tell you the love story of your dad and me.
It's fitting that I write this while sipping a margarita
by the flames of a fire in our chiminea on the back
patio with Stoney in my lap. Nathan and I bonded
initially over margaritas; we share a profound love
for being outside, especially near fire or water; and,
we only have Stoney in our lives because your dad
was thoughtful and kind enough to suggest we find a
way to rescue cats despite his severe allergy to them.

At the writing of this letter, I met your dad just
over eleven years ago. One of my favorite musicians
who had come to be a dear friend, Jimmy LaFave,
had hired me to be his assistant and agent so I could
dip my toes in the music business while also teaching
high school English. My first husband and I had
separated. I'd tripped into a rebound relationship
with a guitar player who was sexy in that so-cool-
and-not-very-nice-but-damn-it-sure-feels-good-
when-he-pays-attention-to-you-kind-of-way. I
became one of those girls whose friends could only
shake their heads and wait for the inevitable

heartbreak that comes when someone is clearly just not that into you. I was a mess. Jimmy and I talked nearly every day, and he was tired of hearing about the drama of my being jerked around and continually returning for more. He wanted me to meet some nice people, one Okie in particular he'd only recently met himself. Jimmy grew up partly in Oklahoma and was very proud of anything or anyone to do with "his" state. He introduced me to Nathan at a Folk Alliance Conference in Memphis, Tennessee. If it embarrasses you that your parents met at a folk conference, it shouldn't. It was cool. We were cool, I promise. (Just maybe not as cool as the guitar player.)

After some pleasantries, Nathan asked about the best margaritas in Houston, and I had lots of thoughts on the subject. We knew we had at least one thing in common, so we agreed to kill time in the hotel bar that night over some of the worst margaritas (served in Styrofoam cups because they'd run out of clean glasses) we would ever have together. It didn't matter. We talked and talked, and I quickly gathered he was kind and funny, in addition to being an artsy writer and smart professor with a Ph.D. We went our separate ways the next day—I to Houston and Nathan to Norman. We remained "pen pals," or "email buddies" more accurately.

After months of long-distance friendship, and a lunch date or two when he passed through Houston, that inexplicable switch flipped one night (coincidentally, while swaying to Jimmy's music at a show where we'd met up in Austin). It's a feeling I can't wait for you to experience: that prelude to falling in love. We still joke that I had to be the first one to actually kiss him. We both felt very cautious—given our previous experiences, a significant age difference, and an uncertain future...as we had each only recently risen from the ashes—but I was the slightly less cautious of the two. So even though I had to be the kisser, I *thought* maybe he was happy to be the kissee...and I *knew* it when he read a poem he'd written about the whole thing over the phone to me.

We dated for two years from our respective hometowns, and then I made the big move up to Oklahoma to live with him. Taking that chance of quitting a stable job and moving to a place where I only knew one person was the best decision of my life. While I don't want to encourage you to be too risky, I have found in the last ten years that being open to change (something I never was before) and saying "yes" to crazy possibilities has never let me down. In fact, it's brought me to this moment I just described...in this yard, in this town, with this cat, this fire, this margarita, and this husband.

~Nathan's wife

More on the romance and the reality…

Any real love story involves troubles and trials, some more drastic than others. It's important for me to share with you not just the romance but also the reality of the ongoing and ever-developing story of your dad and me so that you understand our most important relationships aren't always easy. Your dad and I got married seven years ago. At that point, it was no secret to me that Nathan carried a heavy load on his shoulders, but it's a load I'd foolishly hoped would disappear into the shadows of our beaming blossoming bliss. His twenties and thirties were pretty rough on him. Back when he was an up-standing Christian young man, he'd married and had a child. As often happens in young marriages, things fell apart. Although he knew it had to end, the aftermath of divorcing when Sierra was only two—totally cognizant of all the wounds that inflicted throughout the rest of her childhood—nearly broke him. He wanted more for her, and he wanted (an understatement if there ever was one) to be a full-time dad. His own wounds during those decades weren't limited to the imposed distance from his daughter. In the music business and in his personal life, he found himself in some not-so-great relation-ships, and encountered some bad…some really bad…people, along the way.

And then there was me, at a totally different phase in my life and with my own twenty-nine years of experiences that shaped me into someone with a wildly different view of the world from my particular vantage point. As we worked to weave our lives together, we were mostly happy and we were committed. But we were looking through windows that were miles apart, each with loads of our own personal baggage in the overhead compartments. From these two unique vantage points, we fought often and loudly. Even our everyday conversations could be challenging because of our distinctive communication styles: he is slow and careful with words and likes to paint pictures and compose stories; I am matter of fact and can pack thousands of words into a minute or two fully believing it should all make total sense to the listener. (In general, I thought I should make total sense to him...that it'd be so simple for him to just come up and sit with me at my window and enjoy my view.) Our arguments, to say the least, were not very artful. We were guilty of all that "talking at" nobody is ever supposed to do, raging tempers, sarcasm, competing egos.

It took me a while to realize that I wasn't going to chase away the pains and traumas he'd endured, and maybe it took him a while to realize there were things about me he couldn't change. Even when we moved down to Wimberley two years after getting married to begin a new chapter together, the ghosts of his past followed. We'd also developed some unhealthy patterns in order to bridge our differences and protect ourselves—old standbys like walking on eggshells and shutting down when one of us had hurt feelings.

Shortly after our move, your dad hit the road for a long string of readings and performances, and our connection was being challenged in *all* the ways: physically, emotionally, spiritually. Our home started to feel more like my home since I was the one taking care of the yard, the garbage, the mail, everything. When I wasn't doing that, I created fun for myself and went out with friends. Nathan's not a big question-asker, so phone conversations were strained. My own question-asking habit had typically caused him to be defensive, feeling accused or like I was searching for information, so we just ended up not sharing much. He was driving all through California and Wyoming and who knew where else, mostly wishing he was home while I was building "our" life at home without him, wondering what all he was seeing and doing. Normally time alone and away from one another is actually kind of nice, getting a chance to miss the other person and a break from handling the ins and outs of shared space. I agree with Grandma that I wish for you the ability to be peaceful and happy in solitude as much as you are with those you love. Nathan and I both value, and even need, our solitude. Solitude is different than distance, though, and this time we were drifting apart.

I had been more overwhelmed than I recognized by the power he allowed the dark stuff to have, weary of the ways his past pain could bear its teeth out of nowhere when I, or a set of circumstances, inadvertently triggered it. Without knowing it I'd stopped turning to him as my safe soft place, which means I turned to my friends. Some of those friends were men who may or may not have had their own designs (the question of the intentions of others, and whether they even matter, was an ongoing debate between us). Ultimately, all the disagreements and distance and accusations and proclamations hurled at one another came to a crescendo. We were hurting each other; none of it was on purpose or malicious or careless, but it had to stop.

The point is, when we reached the threshold and fully realized what was happening, he didn't flee and I didn't give up. We didn't fall out of love. We recognized we needed to get our shit together. Then…we worked our asses off to do it. There were times when it was so hard to find the patience to try to understand one another, so hard not to yell, hard to admit to ourselves, and especially one another, who we really were and how different we are, and to know what to change and what to accept in each another. It was hard work to grow together, instead of continuing to grow apart, which can often be a much more natural path. It can still be tough, but we're committed to trying every day. I think the key is that we believe the growing we can do together can help us become our best selves. It doesn't hurt to balance all that hard work with a lot of fun, and even if we forgot for a little while, we really like each other and know how to have fun.

And if I were giving an acceptance speech for a relationship award (maybe that should be a thing!), I would thank those few closest friends whom we could actually let into our deep dark places and our therapist whom we're lucky enough to both love and trust. They gave us the support we needed in order to muster the strength and patience to navigate the treacherous time and terrain in a relationship when pheromones have relinquished the role of confident and sure-footed guide, and two people decide they still want to find their way through to a lasting and fulfilling partnership.

Nathan, and the work I've done to love him and understand him and be a good partner to him, has made me a better version of myself. And I'm confident loving me has done the same for him. This is what I want to tell you, my girl. You'll know when it's worth the work. Sometimes it's just not right, and you should flee. But when you do fall in love with someone who is worth it—someone with whom you can build a fruitful, interesting, challenging, inspiring, exciting life—I hope you will not get too scared by the effort it may take to remain in tune to one another, to continue to hold that person's best interests in your mind, to continue to look out for your own, to look for ways you might grow and to encourage and foster the same in him or her.

Love,
Ashley

About your mom...

I love sunsets but am scared of the dark. I rarely
wake for sunrises.
I love to see Hayes Carll play at the Old Quarter
Acoustic Café in Galveston or the Saxon Pub in
Austin or the Mucky Duck in Houston. I hate
stadium concerts and music festivals.
I love short but hard hikes followed by beers with
cheese and mustard sandwiches in the shade.
I hate crowds.
I love friends who, when they come over, first say
hello to Cayenne with a heartfelt scratch before
saying hello to us.
I like older people. I always have.
I love a good porch, especially with chairs that rock
or swing.
I love one-on-one dates with friends. I don't like
dinners at loud restaurants with awkward seating
arrangements and multiple conversations happening
at once.
I love the sound of coyotes, wolves, and whales. I've
only ever actually heard coyotes "live."
I hate the sound of leaf blowers, commercials, loud
trucks, construction, and crying babies.
I love snuggles and hugs.
I hate goodbyes. I'm okay with see-you-soons. Just
not goodbyes.

On brown sugar sandwiches...

You know by now that I'm all about organic, clean, real foods: nourishment that comes directly from the ground, or responsibly from animals, without additives and processing. What you don't know is that I grew up eating Vienna sausages in a can, Oreos, Cheetos and Doritos, and just about anything packed with preservatives and artificial flavors that are designed to make us want them even more. Oh, and how I loved TV dinners with the delicious compartments of mystery meat and two salty sides. My favorite was the Nighthawk "Taste of Texas": a charred meat patty, cornbread, and ranch style beans.

I don't blame Sandy at all for these eating habits. Parents didn't know yet to worry about microwaving plastic or high-fructose corn syrup lurking in packaged foods. Plus, she never allowed us to eat sugary cereals. Endless Oreos and ice cream sundaes, but no sugary cereals! Just Cheerios and Grape-nuts.

On special occasions when I got the late night, or mid-afternoon or after-school, munchies, Mom would make me brown sugar sandwiches: white bread, margarine, and brown sugar microwaved so it all melted together. My mouth waters with the memory of the guilty pleasure. And if Sandy made me one now, I'd eat it up. But of course I can't find an excuse to make one myself—just the idea that we'd ever have a loaf of white bread in the house now is laughable. The only recipe Sandy taught me that I continue to make is clam sauce and spaghetti. While she made home-cooked meals most nights, cooking wasn't her forte, and there weren't a whole lot of other recipes worthy of passing along. There's certainly nothing wrong with clam sauce and spaghetti when you compare it to sugar sandwiches…but it doesn't meet my usual standards for a recipe, what with its lack of fresh vegetables. It is simply canned diced clams, green onions, parsley, spaghetti, salt and pepper. I can't tell you why it tastes so damn good, why it's what I want for my birthday dinner every year or when I'm home alone and get to cook whatever I want to eat in front of the TV. What I can say is that food is a great source of comfort, health, and happiness. Sometimes it's one or the other and sometimes all three. So in addition to all the leafy greens and ancient grains I would feed you, I would also make you a brown sugar sandwich—requiring a special trip to the store for white bread—whenever you need cheering up. I would teach you how to make clam sauce and spaghetti, which would take about two minutes. I might even buy a pack of Oreos from time to time so you can learn if you like to twist or dunk 'em.

~Mom

When the end is nearer...

Sometimes in the middle of the night, when my defenses are down against those anxieties that are more manageable in the light of day, I panic just a little. My stomach churns, and deep breathing fails to calm me. I wonder: what if Nathan dies before I do (he *is* a bit older), and I'm left to finish my life all alone? My parents would be gone. Parker might still be alive, but we don't usually think of siblings as companions and caregivers in old age. I would have friends and relatives, but I wouldn't have *my* family. It would just be me. Not that you, as an adult, would hang out with me all the time. But you would exist, and a lifetime we shared would exist. And if I become feeble, you would be the one to take care of me. Without you, who will drive me to appointments or help me around the house? Who will sit with me while I slip away to whatever's next? These questions are no reason to have a child. Nobody knows what the future holds. I could die in a car accident shortly after giving birth to you, leaving your dad to raise you alone. "What if's" aren't much good to us here and now. I know that. But, my darling, lying there in the dark, I get scared when I think of coming to the end of my wonderful life all by myself.

~ Mom

To a beautiful human,

If only a mother and father could find the perfect things to say throughout a daughter's life to make her feel beautiful in her own skin, with all her unique features, into her teenage and adult years. I'm afraid that body image issues tend to cause people—girls and women, especially—great distress, no matter what their body type or issues may be. From an early age we seem to be wired...or perhaps shaped by a powerful combination of media and peers...to find things to hate about ourselves, to believe that if we could change these things, life would somehow be better.

I've alluded to what I considered my own problem areas when I was younger. I probably can't even remember the full list of features I have at some time in my life hated or actively worked to change, but it would include freckles, skinny legs, bony knees, a chubby chin, an upturned nose, pale skin, dark circles under my eyes, hair in the wrong places, imperfectly shaped eyebrows, large knuckles and veiny hands, a weird belly button that was surgically transformed from an "outie" to an "innie" when I was little, not much of a butt, smallish breasts, and believe it or not the fact that my second toe on each foot is curved.

Many female friends have little patience for my complaining because I've always been thin, and that has meant I'm not to voice any displeasure with my body, because for so many girls, weight is *the* biggest issue—despite the fact that my skinniness never seemed to earn the rewards or attention their curviness did. Being slim in all the right places while still somehow having a firm round butt and perky sizable breasts seems to be the holy grail for women in our culture. Regardless of our shapes and sizes, or how close one may be to that grail, it remains a normal part of being a girl and woman to find things about our bodies to bemoan, put down, or try desperately to change with expensive products, procedures, crazy cleanses, or dangerous diets.

I'm still susceptible to some of these messages, but somewhere along the way, I just decided to love my body. When you think about it, our bodies are miraculous vessels allowing us to enjoy the human experience for a short while. Hating the vessel, the very source of our breath, seems ungrateful, if not toxic. Plus, I can't change my knobby knees, so what good does it do to think nasty thoughts about them every time I'm in shorts? That gets tiresome. What if we reversed the norm? What if instead of regularly putting down our own bodies, we acknowledged and celebrated our unique features to ourselves and out loud with each other (authentically...not in that superficial-posed-look-at-my-sexy-ass-selfie-that-took-an-hour-to-get-just-right kind of way)?

So, darling perfect girl, I just want you to be healthy, to care for your body with nourishment and activity. And I hope you will love every inch of it. Respect it. Be grateful for it. Know your body is a gift. Share it with others only if they deserve that gift. You are beautiful. Though I will never meet you, this is one thing I know. If you can also know that, and see the equal yet different beauty in every human you meet, that would be a dream come true for a mom.

Love,
Mom

Beautiful Little Me

Why should I not sit, every morning of my life, on the hillside, looking into the shining world?

~ Mary Oliver

On blue skies...

The Stanberry family stories and sayings that live through Uncle Parker and me will die when we die, so they too warrant mourning and honoring. It's not that I believe our little family stories, or even our family, are especially significant, but each little life and family does matter. Our stories matter. And this is a story about your grandfather and one of my favorite things about him that I'd hope he'd pass along to you.

Chip is like your dad in that beauty is rarely lost on him. He is sentimental and expressive about it. Sometimes his sappiness evoked the obligatory embarrassed daughter eye roll, but I think I always loved it about him. As far back as I can remember, not a single blue-sky day has passed when he didn't remark with great appreciation, "There is *not a cloud* in the sky." He said it when we sailed on Lake Conroe; he said it when we skied in Colorado; he said it on Saturday afternoons when we played in the front yard. Sometimes, Parker and I would make a game of finding some tiny white wisp of a cloud shortly after he made the proclamation and giggle at him, wondering if the day was now not quite as perfect.

I know I have Chip in me when I'm out in the yard and am so taken with the bright red of a flower or the silhouette of a tree's branches against the winter sky that I feel the urge to go get your dad or take a picture to share with friends. I'm grateful Nathan shares this appreciation of the beauty that is all around, if you just care to notice. He will often try to hide tears in his eyes at the sight of a sunset in the mountains or the golf course by the house where he grew up, just as I will often find myself captivated at the way the sunlight dances on ripples in a creek or on a tiny pink cactus flower in our library window.

Every time I'm under a bright blue sky, I think of my dad and I hear his voice—*not a cloud in the sky*—and it makes me smile.

~Mom

I finally figured out the only reason to be alive is to enjoy it.
                                        ~ Rita Mae Brown

On our lifestyle...

Over wine and cheese on a recent visit to Oklahoma, Grandma read to us from a snippet she'd literally cut from a magazine to share with us. (I think one of her favorite pastimes is piling up articles and excerpts that will bestow upon us all the wisdom we will ever need to have a bountiful organic garden, avoid cancer, cure acid reflux, enjoy a happy marriage, and basically perfect the art of life.) This snippet was about "hygge." We all worked on the pronunciation together for a while. It turns out it's a Danish word for a way of life. Hygge encompasses coziness, comfort, contentment, togetherness, well-being, and not only being in the present, but enjoying the present. American culture is just starting to embrace concepts like meditation and living in the now, likely as a necessary reaction against our popular values and priorities of the last century that have fostered disease and depression.

Historically, our culture has been largely defined by an obsession with work, money, power, stuff, and an almost deliberate unconsciousness. It has become all too common to move through life without

thinking much about what we can't see, let alone
taking the time to enjoy all the beautiful things we
can. We forget to consider and enjoy what little
miracles our lives are. We esteem busy-ness over
contentment, and we think we are supposed to do,
do, do…until we're so worn out, we just want to
spend our weekends mindlessly watching "reality"
TV shows and bragging to our friends about how
little sleep we've had and complaining about how
much we have to *do*!

Your dad and I prefer hygge. To some, it might
sound like the importance we place on doing what
we love, on ultimately enjoying life, is irresponsible
or luxurious. After all, who has time for cocktail hour
every night and hiking trips on weekday afternoons?
The thing is, it's just about choices. Over the years,
our accountant—whose services we only have the
privilege of using because of Grandpa's church
connections—has been known to report to us at tax
time, "Congratulations, you're poor!" We don't feel
poor, though. Somehow, we scrounge together
enough every month to pay our mortgage and bills.
We've found a beautiful home that we can afford,
partly because we're lucky enough to want to live in a
small town in Texas rather than New York City or
even Austin, where the cost of living would limit us
to a dilapidated 300-square foot studio. Your dad
works so hard, but it's difficult for some to under-

stand that he's actually working since he's chosen to make a living as an artist rather than with a "real job." I love teaching, but admittedly my career is not my priority. I work as an inglorious adjunct professor online so that I can "make a living" in a way I enjoy that also frees me up to do other things, to organize my days how I want to. These choices mean when we aren't "making a living," we *are* living: being outside, cooking, writing, traveling and discovering, sitting and sharing in conversation with friends by the fire.

Some days are more hygge-ish than others. Some are more about the tasks that must be completed, the bookings that must be made if Dad's going to make money next month, the toilets of the rental cabins I must clean if I want extra spending money for tickets to see Hayes Carll play. Some days it's harder to enjoy the moment when we're stressing over a doctor's appointment or car repair. Each day has its own character and focus, its own balance of work and play. Regardless of how the days go, though, as the light begins to fade on each of them, Dad and I meet up to prepare a snack, shake up cocktails, and make the big decision... whether to sit out by the fire pit or on the patio or on the front porch or on the couch. Wherever we choose, there will be candles, a little vase of freshly-cut flowers from our yard, and a toast.

A friend once wrote, "Make something. Break something. Or watch the birds sing. These are your only choices." They are all good choices in their own good times. The point is to choose and spend your time deliberately. Whether I'm making a table out of a pallet I've broken apart, or watching the humming-birds suck the nectar out of the sages, or providing feedback to a student that I hope will help them become a better writer, or carefully wording an email that breaks off a plan with someone I've decided I don't need to appease, the point is to do it con-sciously and to revel in the fact that each act is an act of being alive.

Of course, sweetheart, I know how blessed/lucky/spoiled/privileged we've been—with our parents, with the foundation we were given, with our educations, with all of the support we've received. Given what we have been given, though, we have cultivated a life, with gratitude as the most important tool, in which we try to grow contentment and a connection to one another, to the elements, and to what we cannot see. We try to be. here. now. And to make the now as cozy as possible.

It could be wonderful to bring another precious human into our ¾-acre wood, our neck of the "hygge." But I don't know that we could sustain this life with and for you. Trying to be good parents, the risks, the financial pressure, the emotional stress, the lack of rest and quiet could throw it all out of whack. So, I don't know if I could pull off both motherhood and a life of hygge.

Peace,
Mom

About the darker days...

For all my talk and genuine belief in the importance of being happy simply to be alive, it's more difficult on some days than others. If I had followed a different path, the darker days may have been less intense, but I'm not sure they would have been fewer. I believe this in part due to the nature of my first marriage. We had a peaceful and easy life together—two high school teachers with plenty of money and little to argue about. The type of darkness that descended on us was a more pervasive, lasting dullness. As I began to change and grow a little, it became clear he wasn't interested in doing that with me, or he couldn't. In our relationship, the valleys weren't especially deep or scary, but the peaks weren't especially high or inspiring, especially as the years went on. I was bored. And boredom is my personal greatest enemy. (I'm actually currently working to improve my capacity to sit and be comfortable with some amount of it, but *in moments* rather than *with life*.)

Anyway, all this is to say that with each relationship, and each choice about how we want our lives to be, comes some difficulty and drama, except perhaps for the most enlightened among us (and I think it happens for them too, really). Overall, as you can hopefully tell from what I've written to you so far,

I'm quite happy with my choices—with my home, my lifestyle, my partner. On some days, though, in this home with this partner, it feels like a fish and a horse are carving out a life together. I haven't fully sorted out the nuances of that metaphor and it doesn't matter if I'm the fish or horse in the scenario, but the point is that each moves through their environments of water and land very differently. They relate to their own kind differently, let alone one another. They feel pain differently. They even breathe differently. And yet in this case they love each other deeply. If I had understood all this...that there would be times we seem a little alien to one another...eleven years ago when I met your dad, would I have still chosen this life with him? To quote one of Nathan's older poems about relationship, "you gotta pick your shit." Every person and relationship comes with some of it, and you just have to choose what kind. I can tell you today with absolute certainty I do not regret the choice, and I accept the shit that comes along with all the shine.

Still, my impatient tone of voice and practicality can drive him crazy. His reactions to stress can seem overly dramatic and therefore worry me. My desire to plan rubs up against (and not in a sexy way) his total lack of faith in plans. My tendency to overlook the apparently lust-driven motivations of most men confuses him. His willingness, and preference, to keep most people at a distance and foster few friendships confuses me. On our darkest days, when we let the confusion and lack of understanding hover and stew like a thick fog, we can't seem to find each other—one of us is swimming in the murky sea and one is galloping across the hazy plain. And because we love each other, we feel lost and scared, alone in our respective landscapes wondering how to get to each other. When our emotions, tears, or raised voices cause Cayenne to pant nervously at our feet... this is when I really wonder about being a parent. On the very bright side, we do get better and better at returning to one another after moments or days of disconnect or anger or hurt or confusion. We live in the light far more than we dwell in the dark. Plus, I want to be clear that I'm not suggesting one's contentment or fulfillment in life is dictated only, or even primarily, by their partner should they choose to have one. We are ultimately in charge of our own emotions, our own energy, our own adventure.

And while your dad and I continue to choose to have our adventures together, always working to make more of our days diamonds than stones, I wonder about bringing a child into this venture. If we can't help causing our dog anxiety with our outbursts of emotion, how would our times of tension affect you? And then there's the possibility that in addition to the beautiful bond that parenting

can create, the challenges of the experience would
intensify the muddle-ment of our darker days,
making it harder to steer our way out into the light.

~Mom

The fearless ones say yes even when yes is risky, or say no even when no is hard. The fearless ones love deeply and recklessly, even though that is terrifying. The fearless ones walk into a room as if they deserve to be there, even if they suspect they might not.

~ Katherine Stanley Obando

On your twenty-fifth birthday,

You're reaching the age when your brain is finally winding down its development—not that you should feel you have it all figured out or know yourself fully yet (in fact, that would make me a little nervous). You might be starting to figure out what you want to do, what you want your life to be like. Or you might not. Some people your age will be married already; some will have children; some will have chosen their career path they'll stick with forever. If you haven't done any of these things, I'll be relieved.

Being relatively introspective and self-aware, I thought I had myself and my life pretty well figured out at twenty-five, the age when I first got married to a man I'd loved for years. I may have known *some* stuff, but there's no way I could have predicted the winding path that has brought me to where I am at thirty-eight. And that path involved ending some commitments I'd made when I thought I knew...

My biggest wish for you on this birthday is that you will remain open and be fearless. Don't worry about nailing anything down just yet: job, relationship, where home is. On the other hand, this is a time when life generally demands that you take seriously whatever it is you are doing. I wish for you the ability to walk that fine line between doing what you do with determination and passion and keeping an open mind and spirit with regard to where life may take you. I hope you feel fearless moving forward precisely because you have long-lasting, loyal relationships with family and friends you've taken seriously…and because you've built a trust in them and yourself.

As on all your other birthdays, I hope you feel valued and safe. I hope you are continuing to get to know yourself better but also realizing your self isn't the most important thing in the world. I hope, now that you're "all grown up," that Dad and I have become two of your closest confidants, that we can relieve ourselves a little of the parenting burden and now enjoy just knowing you. We'll continue to help you in every way we can as you continue to learn what makes you tick and how to be the best you.

Love,
Mom

To be or not to be a mother...

As you consider the decision to have children, I
wonder if it will be as difficult for you. Some people
just know: they have a consistent deep desire to have
children, or they don't. For most of my friends (and
of course me), it hasn't been that easy. Evolutionary
history and science tell us that men are driven to
spread their genes and women are driven to give
birth and nurture. It can take a really long time for
evolution to catch up with social change and the
cultural reality that it's getting a little crowded around
here. The disparity, for many, plays out as a silent
battle raging inside each individual: thousands of
years of genetic disposition urging us to procreate vs.
the uniqueness of our current situations and
personalities that may give us some pause about
spreading and nurturing our seed.

As women so much of our value and sense of
feminine worth is, often unconsciously, tied up in sex
and mothering. Every woman I've known closely
who has chosen not to have children—due to
fertility issues, age and life circumstances, or pure
preference—has spent years seriously considering
that choice. Some women I know who are mothers
did the same. Some continue to struggle to come to
terms with either decision long after they've made it.
Some struggle more because of pressure from family,

or even strangers, to do what they would have them do. I am lucky never to have been a subject of that pressure, but I've heard stories. It's one thing when parents annoyingly but lovingly wonder aloud when they'll get to be grandparents. What I find shocking, though, are the instances when acquaintances or strangers care so much about another woman's reproduction that they feel compelled to question or comment on it, again aloud...like she's not an actual woman until she's chosen to change everything about her body and life in order to become a mother, like this is the only role that will truly give her existence any real significance. Personally, I find it easy to dismiss the opinions of those who see the world in black and white and cannot perceive all the beautiful shades of gray in between. But again, I haven't been the target of these questions and comments, so I can't speak to how it feels.

Some women accuse themselves (or others) of being selfish for deciding motherhood may not be the right path for them. I've flippantly used that word myself: "I'm too selfish to have kids. I'm not ready for the sacrifices that come with parenting." This issue of selfishness might be better understood by again turning to a different language. As I learned from Elizabeth Gilbert—spiritual seeker, traveler, and writer—the Mandarin language has two words for what we only have the word "selfish" to describe.

One word means doing what is beneficial to you, and the other means doing what is greedy or cruel. Perhaps it's not "selfish" to make a well-thought-out decision not to bring a child into the world. Perhaps it is realistic and thoughtful. Your dad and I, along with other sensitive and nurturing men and women who have chosen not to have kids, have noted the irony in the fact that often it's the people who care *so* much, who are so *not* selfish, who decide that there's already plenty around us that needs our attention, care, and love...and that without a whole lot of people providing it, the world will become more and more unfit for any child.

It's tough to sort out all the voices: societal expectations, familial expectations and tradition, historical trends, medical advice, the ubiquitous media, and our own intuition. I'm quite certain that no matter the challenges you face in making the decision, you'll make the right one. There really isn't a wrong one, if you've acknowledged it is a choice, to be made deliberately. There is no "wrong" if you are mindful—you can contribute positively and give your love any way you choose.

From one woman to another,
Mom

To a child of this planet,

As a species, one of our contributions to the planet is something called the Great Pacific Garbage Patch. It's what it sounds like: a massive pile of trash floating out in the middle of the ocean. We've played a similarly destructive role with the skies and lands, emitting so much toxicity into the atmosphere that we've depleted the ozone layer and caused an unnaturally rapid warming of the planet. In other words, our ignorance, unconscious and uncompassionate behavior—our unwillingness to consider the whole if it means that our part is slightly less easy or affluent—is likely to someday lead to the demise of the human race, if not the entire planet.

By the way, I'm quite aware Al Gore explains this much more accurately and eloquently than I. Regardless, though, of the scientific facts or predictions, it's pretty obvious that we've taken quite a toll on this glorious spinning sphere we call home.

I am a guilty contributor to the problem. Most of us are. Dad and I are mindful of how much waste we create, how much we emit into this delicate environment, and how much we destroy in our paths. Though being mindful in and of itself doesn't keep us from failing on a regular basis. I'm telling you all this because it's yet another contradiction I can't sort out when I consider parenting. Raising a child would add to my sense of responsibility—to the earth and to you—but could also exacerbate the problem. Maybe it will be too damn hard and gross to use cloth diapers instead of adding disposable ones to the landfills three to four times a day (or do babies make their little messes even more often than that?). Maybe you will rebel against your hippie-ass parents and become an adult who cringes at the phrase "carbon footprint."

Sometimes it's already so overwhelming to consider how many billions of people there are and how few realize, how we all realized too late, that it matters how we move through this world, what we put in and what we take out. It's overwhelming to consider my own role in all this, let alone the shaping of another's role. And I can't even begin to wrap my mind around the possibility that just one generation away, the damage we've done will start to show itself in even scarier ways, making your great big home unstable and unsafe.

~Eco-Mom

Silence of the heart is necessary so you can hear God everywhere—in the closing of the door, in the person who needs you, in the birds that sing, in the flowers, in the animals.

~ Mother Teresa

On my immortality project...

Part of the grieving process of opting out of parenthood is accepting that I'm not leaving behind a definitive legacy. I am not creating anything out of my DNA to carry on the blood of my family. The imprint I make is left to me alone. When I take the time to think about it, though, not raising a child doesn't actually mean any person's existence, or legacy, or "immortality" is compromised. It's interesting, in fact, to consider why and how the concept of legacy is important to us.

Ernest Becker, a philosophical anthropologist, was fascinated with how our terror of death defines and drives our behaviors as a species...not always in productive or beneficial ways. He had his own take on selfishness. He posited that our efforts to protect or extend our existence—through children, or the creation and building of things that will last past our deaths—are not only selfish, but can border on evil. Good and evil aside, it's part of the human condition to seek to have meaning, and understand what that meaning is, in the "grand scheme of things." I'm no exception. But as Becker believed, perhaps that meaning can come from tapping into my own divinity. Whether I bear children, or get a building dedicated to me (hahaha), or create a work of art that outlasts me, perhaps our real immortality project lies in understanding our inherent connection to the universe. And if we can't perceive that, maybe that's when we're susceptible to misguided efforts and "evil" deeds.

I do want you to know that no matter how many philosophical ways there are to spin it, I take my decision not to have you seriously, and I will strive to honor you with the life I lead without you. I used to say that I'd either have kids or horses. I was only sort of joking: they both involve a major commitment of time and money, and I knew I couldn't invest in both. I don't know that I'll ever "own" horses in lieu of having you, but I'll never ignore the voice inside that's always called me to help animals. Maybe I can even help people by fostering their relationships with animals. It's my dream to run an animal sanctuary for the most neglected, abused, or "unadoptable" animals, whether horses, rabbits, dogs, goats, or donkeys. I envision many ways that sanctuary could be a refuge of sorts for people too. Even if the dream doesn't come to fruition, I promise to you that I will devote myself to nurturing and saving any animal life I can, to inspiring any one person I can to realize the value in kindness, to lessening pain and suffering. That is an imprint I can make.

Dad and I also believe in words and stories. We have built a little publishing company together, with a mission to publish the poetry and stories of musicians who have found they have more to say than a song can contain. With our group of artists and authors, we hope to tell and share good stories, stories that speak to the complexity of our existence, to the truths that are worth exploring. Maybe another human will read those words someday, and a life will be impacted. We will also always make and grow things: music, sculptures, flowers, food, furniture, books, fires, friendships. We will listen to the silence, and we will seek out what the rocks, waters, air, and earth have to tell us and respect what we learn from them. As little as that may be, angel, I think it's something.

Honoring you,
Ashley

50 things I will miss doing with you:

1. Singing and rocking you to sleep.
2. Making you laugh.
3. Sitting with you while Stoney purrs in your lap.
4. Walking through the woods with only your observations to break the silence.
5. Having a picnic and dozing on a blanket in the shade of the trees.
6. Watching you touch the velvety nose of a horse.
7. Dancing.
8. Cooking clam sauce and spaghetti.
9. Taking you to new places that I'll see for the first time along with you.
10. Making Dad homemade birthday cards together.
11. Being woken up by you on Christmas morning, too excited to wait.
12. Planting vegetables in the garden.
13. Taking you for visits with Chip and watching his face light up when he sees you.
14. Taking you to volunteer at an animal shelter.
15. Baking a cake from scratch for my first time ever on your sixth birthday (it seems like a good year for that).
16. Reading to you. Anything and everything. Any time.
17. Watching you and Dad make pancakes together.
18. Playing I Spy.

19. Giving you your own stuffed "Rabby" to wear thin with love.

20. Teaching you sun salutations and practicing them together in the mornings.

21. Snuggling you up in a warm soft towel after a bubble bath.

22. Sipping martinis together when you're old enough.

23. Taking you on a trip, just the two of us like my dad did, for your sixteenth birthday (Nathan can take you on another one).

24. Scratching your back.

25. Holding your tiny hand.

26. Learning from you what unconditional love, the willingness to die for another, feels like.

27. Playing CDs of Jimmy LaFave and all the other really good ones for you…the stuff you don't hear on the radio.

28. Learning from you how to be better and do better and listen better.

29. Making a snowman the first time you see snow.

30. Teaching you how to arrange flowers we've picked and candles and pretty things in our home.

31. Watching you and your dad sing a song together, maybe while you strum along on your own little guitar.

32. Forming a family band (only sort of kidding).

33. Creating a cozy fort on a rainy night, with squishy pillows and soft blankets and twinkle lights and special snacks.

34. Feeling your hand hold mine as I leave this planet.

35. Taking you to sit with Grandma in her art studio while she paints.

36. Comforting you with my cool hand on your forehead when you are sick or have woken up from a nightmare.

37. Making your birthdays and Christmases magical.

38. Bundling you up with mittens and a hat on those (rare) cold blustery days.

39. Taking road trips.

40. Hearing the observations and statements only a child can make, the ones that may seem silly or otherworldly or out of nowhere...the ones that often hold the truth.

41. Picking you up from school on a gloomy day and making hot chocolate together in our sweats.

42. Napping.

43. Roasting marshmallows (or veggie hot dogs, or something healthier) in the fire around the beautiful stone fire pit area your dad has made.

44. Seeing how Nathan and I show up in your face.

45. Sitting outside drawing or writing in journals together...being together, but doing our own thing.

46. Taking turns thinking of random acts of kindness we could do for people.

47. Witnessing what an amazing father Nathan would be to you.

48. Listening to how you and Sandy talk, and seeing my own mom with a little girl again.

49. Cheering you on in whatever sport, performance, or activity you love.

50. Cheering you on in life.

I need you to rise above
and fill your world with love
as you move around the great big universe.
In the click of a photograph
it all passes way too fast,
and when your part is cast,
there's no time to rehearse.
May all your joy by true.
That's what I wish for you
as you're traveling the roads of the earth.

~ Jimmy LaFave

What I don't know, what I believe, and what I know:

I don't know why we are here. I don't know what happens to us when we die. I don't know if soul mates exist, if certain people's lives or spirits are destined to intertwine. I don't know if destiny itself exists, if things happen for a reason or if everything is as it should be. I don't know if I have been the best daughter, friend, or wife I could be…but, I try. I don't know how many of my decisions have been "right" or "wrong." I don't know what goes on in the mind of Cayenne as we walk together or look each other in the eyes. I don't know, really, what goes on in the mind of any other person or animal.

I don't know what causes cancer. I don't know if wine is killing us or saving us. I don't know how to hear the angels...but, I'm always trying. I don't know exactly, or at all, what angels are. I don't know what will happen next. I don't know why it's so hard to stop wondering and worrying about what will happen next. I don't know if I will regret not having you.

I believe that everything and every creature is made up of energy that is all connected. I believe life is basically made up of this energy, love, and music. I believe our brains, most of ours, are only capable of comprehending about one billionth of what is real and true. I believe if I were to learn how to be still in silence more that I would start to know more. I believe religions that place judgment and absolute "truths" above compassion, love, and acceptance cause more harm than good. I believe we should enjoy as many hours of our temporal lives as we can, and that our enjoyment honors the bodies and times we've been given. And I believe it's easier to enjoy life when we recognize our littleness while also recognizing our divinity, revel in daily pleasures we can bestow upon one another and ourselves, make stuff, and love openly and fearlessly. I believe in the power of gratitude.

ௐ

Disclaimer: I use the word "know" knowing that I don't really know anything. I suppose knowing is just a step beyond believing. So, this is what I *really* believe…

I know there is so much more—so much more in this universe than can be seen or explained. I know that just the right amount of vodka is always better than a little too much. I know this is true of most pleasures, even cheese. I know my family and friends have made my life extraordinary. I know everybody messes up. I know forgiveness matters. I know every breath I take—every giggle, every sigh, every tear—is a gift, and from "whom" doesn't matter. I know I knew things as a little girl that I wish I could remember to know now. I know life would be beautiful with you. And I know it will be beautiful without you. I know you're out there no matter what. In ways words cannot say.

With all my love,
The Mother You'll Never Have

Epilogue

So I have found myself at age thirty-eight childless by choice and, barring some unforeseen surprise or massive shift, remaining that way. After leaving my job as a teacher to live with Nathan, I had both the luxury and courage to begin to imagine a life that didn't revolve around what I "do" professionally. I was able to consider a lifestyle and career that didn't include sleep deprivation, dreaded faculty meetings under florescent lights, and cafeteria lunches. I paid attention to what lit me up and gave me energy and to what drained it. Now, after going back to school and earning a graduate degree, I teach online Humanities courses for the University of Oklahoma's College of Professional and Continuing Studies. Together, Nathan and I run the publishing company he brought to life years ago, and I work as an editor and freelance writer. And...I clean rental cabins in town. Yep, I'm a professor and a maid. And outside of the occasional sloppy inconsiderate vacationer who leaves a cabin a mess, or the occasional student who illustrates zero effort or attention to feedback, I love every minute of it. I love waking up at 10 a.m., setting an alarm only when I need to get up a little earlier to beat the heat on a horseback ride. I love that I can take a road trip whenever I want, as long as there's wi-fi. I love spending most of my time in yoga pants...even if I used to make fun of those people. I love not having to show up at a school or office but still getting to do work that feels important, and that I'm able to take a break from grading papers by heading outside to check on the cats and pick weeds from the vegetable garden. And I love living in Wimberley...I'll come back around to that in a moment.

Years ago, I encouraged Nathan to give up classroom teaching at OU to commit fully to what he is at his core: a writer, musician, and performer. He still teaches but he teaches small intensive creativity workshops all over the country that he enjoys rather than university courses that strain his eyes (all the grading!) and interfere with his ability to travel and tour. That travel—the readings, concerts, and workshops—means we're often apart. Mostly it's a perfect juxtaposition of weeks when we're both working from home, able to spend every evening with one another and enjoy the occasional afternoon nap together or jaunt into town during the day, with chunks of days or weeks away from one another. The separation and transitions (leaving, returning, leaving, returning) can be challenging, but damn I love making myself dinner at 9:45 p.m. and leaving the TV on all day even when I'm not watching, and

Nathan loves driving back roads alone in silence (I always have music on) and the thrill of reading and singing for people. We like missing each other, although I know he covets the occasional role reversal when he would get to stay in our home alone and I would be the one to go.

We found our home in Wimberley after house-hunting for a year, loosely searching for a quiet and beautiful place to live where we could be close enough to venture into Austin to see our friends play music or meet up for brunch or birthday dinners or whatever celebration is in order. We wish we could have afforded acreage—one necessary step to bringing an animal sanctuary to fruition—but we often pause to reflect on how amazing what we *could* afford is: a comfortable home with a library/writing room for Nathan and office for me, a big backyard that has at least become a sanctuary for our cats Stoney and Dylan if not goats and horses, a community with plenty of people who love art and music, savor peace and quiet, and drink a lot of wine. We like where our life is, and we like the direction it seems to be heading. But...

As a chronically indecisive person, I have a hard time deciding what vegetable or shrub to plant where (I will spend an hour just staring, starting a hole, having second thoughts, staring some more); which friend to call when; whether or not I want to drive into Austin for a night out or save money and stay home in comfy sweats; if I want to commit a half-day to taking my friend's horses out for a trail ride or not; what to order on the rare occasion we dine out; what home to buy; whether to give Cayenne antibiotics for a cough or to stick with homeopathic remedies. Sometimes the little anxious butterflies that come with (or cause?) the indecision are brought on by the thought that I don't have enough information to *know* what I *should* do. Sometimes they flutter around in there because I worry about making others happy and not only have to figure out what will do that but must measure it against my own best interests. Other times I don't want to miss out on the thing I'm not choosing. All that indecision and cyclical thinking about being a parent was causing me more pain than deciding to be bold enough to finally say, "I'll never." Nathan is a parent, and I'll never know what that feels like. There are countless experiences I'll never have with my own child. Fully acknowledging them and bringing them into the light has helped to accept them. I'm at peace with what will never be.

My Sarah is pregnant now. She has always wanted to be a mom, and because her memory is better than mine, she's reminded me that even when we were young, we were fascinated by the fact that she *knew* she wanted children, and I didn't know one way or the other. I've witnessed how sure she's been along the way—in preparing to get pregnant, in learning the news, in dealing with the nausea and exhaustion, in finding out she's having a boy, all while the circumstances for being pregnant and having a baby are less than ideal, since her husband has gone back to school and she's in the early stages of her counseling career and money is tight to say the least. She wants this child so badly. And I'm so happy for her. Admittedly, I've been a little relieved that I've not felt pangs of envy or had second thoughts as my best friend in the world begins the adventure of motherhood. I will continue to witness it, and be blown away by it, and relieved I'm not the one embarking on the adventure. I will be thrilled to be an "aunt" to her little boy.

Sarah has been my number one sounding board and supporter as I've written these letters. The conversations we've had over our lifetime about what we each want and need have helped hugely in understanding that different people have different natures, and different ways of nurturing. The writing of the letters also led to many enlightening, and sometimes confusing, conversations with my family members. Confusing only because my in-laws, my parents, and even Nathan all see the same "pros and cons" and we can all get caught up in the back-and-forth between them. I am grateful to have parents and parents-in-law who have helped me sort out my feelings, and grateful for how these letters have sparked conversations with them about their own experiences as parents. My sweet mother-in-law confessed she "scolded" her boys on the occasions when all three of them just became too much, recalling her mortification when she realized a deacon from their church had overheard one of these occasions, as if she had anything to be ashamed of. My ever-patient and calm father-in-law confessed to multiple instances of having to "pull this car over" to reprimand (perhaps with some light threatening?) the misbehaving boys. Knowing them as I do now, it was hard to envision them ever losing their temper. As ridiculous and unnatural as I know it is, I had always imagined their family lived in a constant and perfect state of harmony and serenity. I enjoyed hearing these stories and getting to know my in-laws more fully through them.

My mom and I talked candidly about the best and worst of pregnancy and parenting. I emailed her often to ask about her memory of stories from my childhood. She emailed me black and white photos of her parents when they were young. She told me stories about her own childhood. Even now, we both revel in relief at all the complications I'm not inviting into my life while simultaneously grieving as we wonder what to do with the baby clothes she saved for my little girl. I appreciate that together we can settle into that gray area where relief and grief meet.

My dad was very eager to read an early draft of the letters, and doing so led to some lovely long conversations at his kitchen table. He assured me he felt no sense of loss in not being a grandfather and that the concept of keeping the family name alive didn't matter much to him—these were not things I ought to worry about. He wanted to make sure money wasn't a serious factor in preventing me from having a child if I really wanted to, because he would help there. He sympathized with the difficulty I'd clearly had in making the decision because it has never been black or white: a major urge to parent or an absolute disinterest in it. He realized the indecision itself had been painful, an astute observation, and hoped that pain has diminished throughout this process. It has. He told me how happy and proud he is that I've carved out a beautiful, slightly non-traditional life for myself with Nathan. And as he choked up, he told me parenting was the absolute best experience of his life, the best thing he'd done, and that he was sorry for that reason that he and my mom hadn't been able to keep our family together, for the sake of my brother and me.

It was therapeutic to have all these conversations with my family—to learn how they felt as parents and to feel their love knowing they all only want my happiness and what is best for me. I wrote the letters in part to express the values I'll never share with or pass along to a child, but in doing so I had the wonderful surprise and satisfaction of sharing and discussing those values with my family that's here now. My conversations about the letters with Nathan also brought us closer. We laugh together when, all in one day, we'll look at each other wistfully when an adorable gentle little girl asks to pet Cayenne on a walk, and then look at each with thankful smiles when we witness a toddler screaming in the grocery store while his mother tries not to lose her mind.

I hope these letters continue to inspire conversations. I hope other women and men who are working to make, or have made, the decision to be or not to be a parent feel at peace with whatever their decision is. Let us acknowledge the sense of wonder about what we're missing or what would have been and also celebrate all of the love, care, and nurturing we have to give the life that exists all around us… parents or not.

Acknowledgements

I am grateful to my early readers who provided thoughtful feedback and encouragement: Sarah Hernandez, Kellie Salome, Rod Picott, Lise Liddell, Sarah Flournoy, Liz McIlravy, and my editor Tiffany Yates Martin...who helped me dig deeper.

Mary Lancaster, thank you for telling me "they" wanted this book published.

Chris Everett, thank you for making the outside so beautiful.

Mom and Dad, thank you for the magical childhood you made possible, for being the best parents I could ask for, and for your unconditional love and support.

Parker, thank you for all the ways you shaped that magical childhood as my big brother. I've always loved you and have always appreciated your support.

Norma, thank you for bringing the cover to life.

Nathan, thank you...
for telling me for years that you think I'm a writer...
for making this book possible...
for inspiring me...
for the life we've carved out together...
and for being both sad and happy with me about the child that life is missing.

MEZCALITA
PRESS

An independent publishing company
dedicated to bringing the printed poetry,
fiction, and non-fiction of musicians who
want to add to the power and reach
of their important voices.

CPSIA information can be obtained
at www.ICGtesting.com
Printed in the USA
FFHW02n1744110918
48332899-52152FF